SURVIVE THE ODDS

FORECASTING THE HEALTH
OF YOUR BUSINESS
USING CUSTOMER ANALYTICS

Keith Aichele

Published by Misaic Group, LLC

Survive the Odds

Forecasting the Health of Your Business Using Customer Analytics

First Edition

Copyright © 2014 by Keith Aichele

Published by Misaic Group, LLC

ISBN: 978-0-578-13953-1

PREFACE

I've always found entrepreneurship to be extremely fascinating. For me, it's not just about working for yourself, but the idea of creating something new, exciting and different for the marketplace is such a rush. It can be simple too. My brother used to laugh at me as back in college I would sell scoops of Kool-Aid to my dorm floor. And yes, I mean actual Kool-Aid, nothing else; although I did expand that further into snack goods as I realized the margins that could be made by buying in bulk.

Adding to my little vending shop came the rental of my powered scooter. By reserving a time on the paper taped to the outside of my door, along with some cash, and the keys to the scooter could be yours for an hour or two. You'd be surprised what "broke" college kids will pay so they don't have to walk to class. Thank goodness no one ever got hurt because I didn't even think about the liability of such an endeavor.

To close the income needs, I spent my free time tutoring students attending school through special programs assisting those coming from less fortunate educational backgrounds. This may have been one of the best jobs of my life. Even though there was nothing innovative about being a tutor, although my teaching style could be an area of differentiation, the ability to set my own hours, control my income, and at the same time, feel as though I was really making a difference in people's lives...nothing could be

i

better. It was in that moment that I confirmed entrepreneurship was for me.

Despite the desire to own my own business, I was sucked into corporate America by a well-paying job offer waiting for me upon graduation. The thought of buying a real car sounded fantastic. While the corporate world is a completely different path from entrepreneurship, it was still a worthwhile journey as it provided me amazing business skills and insights - especially being fortunate to have worked for the global leader in marketing research and information.

After a few years into my corporate gig, I found my next innovative idea (many came before this which are fun to share over some drinks). With the internet just starting to take off, I found a way to leverage my business and technical skills to jump on this emerging trend, launching a new business completely on my own. Working full time in corporate and launching a startup simultaneously meant putting graduate school on hold; but when you work for yourself you can decide if you require an MBA or not to run the company.

Faster than I could imagine, the business hit a tipping point - either I needed to hire someone to try and run it, or I needed to leave the corporate job behind and do it myself. So, I took the ultimate plunge. I cashed out the ten thousand dollars I had accrued in my 401k, my only savings, and went for it. Oh, by the way, I had a mortgage, two cars, a two year old daughter, and my wife made minimal income in child care. So, it was all up to me to keep things afloat...on ten thousand dollars.

With determination, passion and persistence, this small business I dreamt up became the industry leader in the Chicago marketplace within 18 months, and put me in a position to sell the company after just 5 years; the same point at which the majority of new ventures have closed their doors. Before the age of 30, I reached a level of financial success that I could only dream of previously.

The entire experience was one of the most exciting and rewarding journeys of my professional life. During that time I was able to connect with so many small business owners, many of whom continued to struggle. I empathized with the tremendous amount of time, energy, passion and focus that owning a small business takes, despite the level of success experienced. I felt bad for those who struggled, as my hard efforts were paying off and theirs were not.

After moving on from my successful venture, I decided I wanted to help others be successful too and formed my current company Misaic. I studied small businesses closely to identify what I did differently to achieve success that could make an impactful difference for others. Outside of the marketing, analytic, and strategic guidance that my background in corporate and personal ventures brought to my clients, I realized that there were key tools missing for small businesses to enable them to act on strategies that resulted from business consulting sessions. So rather than just providing guidance on how to be more successful, I developed a technology platform to provide tools that enable businesses to act tactically, making the consulting recommendations all the more valuable.

How does that bring us to this book? At Misaic, we bring our passion and experience to provide the knowledge and tools needed to implement business health monitoring and activate customer analytics with our clients, as these are critical differentiators I've found to enable success. We cover more ground than is even mentioned in this book. Helping businesses alter their future for the better is incredibly rewarding; however, the reality is Misaic cannot reach every small business. But that does not mean that every small business should not have a fighting chance to overcome the massive failure rates plaguing small businesses everywhere. So, in thinking about how I could expand the reach of the Misaic mission, "helping small businesses achieve sustainable success", it was clear that finding a way to share the concepts of business health monitoring broadly would provide a solution.

I undoubtedly believe that if a business owner or leader can understand and implement the concepts of this book, they will drastically improve their odds of success. For some businesses, this book can mean the difference between success and failure, enabling the owner to live out his or her dream of entrepreneurship. For others, this book will drive success to a higher level than otherwise achievable. In either case, my time and effort writing this book has paid off and the Misaic mission is achieved.

Finally and most importantly, from my own experience, I recognize that the impact of business success goes beyond the owner, extending to their family, employees and employee's families. This book is my personal attempt to make a noticeable impact in the lives of many small business owners and those that surround them.

TABLE OF CONTENTS

INTRODUCTION

How do you do it? How do you prevent the precious entity that you've poured endless amounts of energy, thought, and capital into from becoming nothing more than a "remember that company..." – that is, if you're lucky enough to even be remembered?

The bad news: there is no magic bullet to prevent it. When you launch a business, you start at day one with the odds stacked against you. The good news: this book will show you how to shift the odds in your favor. Though it will require a bit of effort, anyone serious about having a sustainable and successful business can do it. The small amount of time investment to implement the strategies in this book can put your business on the path to long term success.

So what's going to make the greatest impact to your business? What am I suggesting here that most small businesses are missing? The idea is simple. Your business needs proper health monitoring. That's right. You need to continuously measure and forecast the health of your business. To that point, I've developed a mathematical formula that nearly every business can use to determine if they are on a long term path of success, and then alter the path of their business for the better using this information. Even if your company is already healthy, this formula can be used to make your business even healthier and sustain your success. For those of you saying "I already measure the health of my business", let me clarify a critical difference between the measurement I'm referring to vs. typical accounting measurement, as this can be the key difference between success and failure. But before I do, let's make sure everyone recognizes the importance of measuring your business health.

The Health Parallel

The importance of understanding the health of your business is no different than understanding your personal health. When you go for a routine physical, your doctor checks for signs and symptoms that something may be wrong, even if you currently feel great. Prime examples are blood pressure and cholesterol level tests. Both of these tests can reveal hidden conditions that you would never recognize without the proper regular monitoring. Such conditions are associated with heart disease, the #1 killer of men and women in America, resulting in 1 out of 3 deaths. Now, many people are fortunate to survive a heart attack, but the damage itself can often be disabling. Oddly enough, many people who have heart attacks are unaware of hidden conditions such as high blood pressure or cholesterol that could have easily been treated in advance to reduce the risks. For these folks, a simple routine exam may have saved their life.

At the same time, there are those who are aware of their conditions but fail to take proper medication, eat healthy and/or exercise as recommended by physicians to reduce the odds.

Having the knowledge of unhealthy conditions is only half the equation...to make a difference, you must take action as well.

Just the same, most businesses operate without fully understanding hidden conditions that can result in business downturn. In some cases, a business can catch a problem in time to stay afloat for a bit longer, but that is a very stressful and often unsatisfying journey. In the extreme case, this can result in a Chapter 11 bankruptcy where the company attempts to restructure its debts and fight for survival. Other times, it's too late and the business must dissolve.

What if as a business owner or leader, you could identify such hidden conditions in advance? What if rather than waiting for disaster to strike, you could take action early to avoid any downturn or minimize the impact? The good news is that you can, and this book will show you how. As I mentioned before, there is a very precise formula that can be computed that indicates the overall health of your business. Before I move on to explain what makes this health monitoring different, I want to emphasize again that knowledge is only the first part of the equation. To be successful, you must take appropriate action to address the problem once it's identified. To avoid ending up like the heart attack patient who knew about risk factors yet chose not to exercise, you must act on your knowledge to reap the benefits.

Why Financial Statements Are Not Enough

Before getting into details on the health monitoring I'm recommending, let me first explain why using financial statements is not sufficient to ensure the survival of your business. When I

3

refer to financial statements, I'm referring to your typical accounting based reports that describe the financial state of your business. At the most basic level, this could be your bank statements showing your account balances, including a trend of your cash balances over the past few months. If you've taken a basic accounting class or have an accountant helping you with your books, your financial statements will be a bit more sophisticated including an income statement, statement of cash flow, balance sheet (showing assets and liabilities), etc.

These are all very important pieces of information and should never be foregone. In fact, content from these statements will be inputs to the formula used to measure your business health. However, these alone are not comprehensive enough to be predictors of future performance and success. These articles are merely snapshots of "how your business feels". You must dissect the business further to understand the factors that drive the financial numbers for the current period and beyond.

To illustrate this further, let's use a very extreme example that can provide clarity in how looking purely at financial statements can be misleading to long-term business sustainability. Let's consider two independent real estate agents, Bob and Susan. Looking at their latest financial picture, their businesses appear rather similar as outlined in the table below:

	Susan	Bob
Business Savings	6,500	7,200
Rent & Utilities	1,300	1,200
All Other Expenses	400	300

	Susan	Bob
Revenue Last Month	7,000	6,500
Revenue Past 12 Months	62,000	71,000
Outstanding Debts/Liabilities	0	0
Monthly Salary/Distribution	5,000	5,000
Years of experience	2	10

Notice they have about the same amount of revenue, expenses, and savings. They each pay themselves a $60k annual salary to live on. The main difference between the two is that Bob has 10 years of experience while Susan only has 2 years. Now, what if I told you that 3 months after this snapshot Bob went out of business and Susan continued on with only a slight decline in her revenue? That's right, just 3 months later Bob's business completely went under. So what happened? What's missing in this picture that the typical financial statements didn't call out?

Well, here's what happened. Bob and Susan both had strong relationships with ABC Mortgage Experts, one of the leading mortgage companies in the area. ABC had been around for nearly 20 years. Bob, when he started his business 10 years ago, began working with ABC to generate the primary source of his cliental. He was their preferred agent since he knew the original founder of the company. He never had any issues generating enough clients to meet his monthly revenue goals. Susan, however, had only been in the business for 2 years. So, while she had some loan officer relationships at ABC, she was forced to establish relationships with several mortgage companies. ABC only represented 20% of her business, while it was 80% of Bob's.

Furthermore, Bob was very focused and worked hard for his customers to help them find a home, which people appreciated. However, once a customer contracted on their new home, Bob figured he's getting paid no matter what, and would become quite unresponsive to calls. As a result, almost none of his customers would come back to him for their next home purchase. Susan, on the other hand, provided a phenomenal experience from start to finish; and not only would go on to gain future business from most of her customers, she earned their referrals as well.

Now, going back to what happened. Over the three months following the time of the financial picture we reviewed, ABC Mortgage Experts went out of business. You can already see what happened. Bob's primary source of business just disappeared. And, he did not have enough cash reserves to take him through the 'startup period' of finding a whole new set of clients, just as a new agent that enters the industry would have to do.

What was missing from the financial picture, and typical financial pictures, is the understanding of the key drivers and metrics that influence the monthly financials. In this particular example, it would have been important to understand the customer acquisition rates/costs as well as customer retention/attrition rates. Knowing these metrics and their impact on the business sustainability could have allowed Bob to prevent this type of catastrophe from happening.

Now, while this example may appear a bit extreme, simple, and obvious, the purpose of including it was to demonstrate the importance that other metrics play in determining sustainability beyond what a financial statement can provide, no matter how simple or complex the situation is. In fact, intuition may have suggested that, with just the financial picture presented, Bob would have a greater chance of survival over Susan, having been in the business for 10 years vs. 2 years. But that was certainly not the case. The message is hopefully clear - financial statements alone are not enough!

Proper Health Monitoring

I remember asking one of my clients how he measures the success of his business and his response was "I just check to see if there's money left in the bank at the end of the month." To be clear, I do not recommend this approach as an optimal way to measure your business health.

As I mentioned previously, there is a difference between the type of business monitoring that comes directly out of your accounting software versus the type of monitoring I'm suggesting is required to preserve your company. Looking at financial statements is simply recognizing symptoms. It does not necessarily identify the root causes of either success or failure. We can often generalize that the business is growing because sales are up or costs are down, but that's not enough. You need to point to elements that are even more actionable, versus just seeking top line figures.

As we progress through this book, it's important to understand what I mean by a healthy business. I have found that success and sustainability come down to the following principle: a business is successful and healthy when it can consistently produce greater revenue than its expenses. It's really that simple. Forget looking at financial statements that claim the business has value because of assets and "net worth". Or furthermore, cash flow statements which include financing activities which just result in acquiring more debt. Leave that for the accountants for a different purpose and focus on a view that actually has a direct relationship and predictability to your business's sustainability. Turn your focus to a health rating that has one sole purpose – determining the viability of your company.

So, here they are, the metrics of health monitoring that will differentiate your business from the competition and all the other businesses that will continue down the path of fighting against the odds:

- Customer Acquisition Cost
- Customer Acquisition Rate
- Total Number of Customers
- Direct Revenue Per Customer
- Customer Attrition
- Operating Cost
- Total Cash Invested/Available
- Inventory

That's it. These 8 metrics in some form or variant together, along with a mathematical algorithm, can provide a powerful forecast to put the odds of success in your favor. If any of these concepts or metrics appear daunting to you, don't worry. We're going to explore each one of these in detail and walk through how to compute these critical metrics.

My guess is that even if you know these terms, you may not actually be collecting this information or producing these metrics as part of your regular business practice. And if you happen to be collecting these, you're likely not incorporating these into a continuous health monitoring process. Why do I say this? I researched more than 30 small businesses, varying by industry, revenue, size, and time in business, and found that less than 13% of businesses are regularly tracking (if even at all) the critical customer metrics required to fuel the health monitoring equation. Of the businesses that actually track the right metrics, only half believed that they have a significant understanding of the health of their business; indicating that they're likely not fully leveraging their information. Furthermore, despite the low percentage of businesses collecting the required metrics, more than 55% of all businesses believed they had at least a sufficient understanding of their business health. It is this type of disconnect that I believe leads to the common failure rate of businesses. For more information on the research study, see Appendix B.

The Customer Focus

You may have noticed that 5 of the 8 metrics include the term "customer" in their name. That's right. There needs to be a very heavy focus on the customer to determine the health of your business. While this may seem daunting, especially if you feel as though you know nothing about your customers today, it should not be a surprise. In fact, I believe this is another contributor as to why so many businesses, big and small, fail; lack of focus on customer analytics. Companies are so busy just trying to keep up with the daily grind that there never appears to be time to focus on customer analytics. Yet most companies would assert, or minimally agree, that customers are the heart of every business. Without customers, there is no business. We can look at bank account balances and inventory all day long, but ultimately, it starts and ends with the customer.

If you do not spend the time to understand your customers, there's a substantial risk that you will not stay in business for long. Understanding customers is a key ingredient to the success of most large organizations. This is why you will find loyalty programs at so many major retailers. They use your shopping behavior to make better, more informed business decisions. Remember the major retailer that was marketing baby products to a high school girl as they knew she was pregnant before her parents did (I won't name the retailer but if you think long enough you'll hit it on the bulls eye). This was all done through a strong understanding of customer purchase behavior.

Many companies don't even know who their customers are, especially in retail establishments where capturing customer details is not common. If you acknowledge that this is true for your business, don't fret. I'm going to show you how to know each and every one of your customers, no matter what industry you're in. And, if you're not already using customer information, you will be ready to by the end of this book, or at least you should be. Only with this proper customer information can you generate the customer analytics that serve as the foundation for proper business health forecasting, which we will discuss in detail throughout. Beyond what is presented here, there are many applications of advanced customer analytics which warrant an entire book on its own (sounds like a foreshadowing to my next book).

What's to Come

Now that I've shared with you the basic metrics that comprise proper business health monitoring and forecasting, hopefully you can identify whether what follows is new to your organization. The remainder of this book is divided into two parts. In part one, we'll walk through the process of gathering your data and creating each of the individual metrics. In this step-by-step process, you'll learn how to leverage the information you might even already have about your customers. And if you're not collecting any customer information, I'll show you how to get started so you can be on your way to properly measuring your business health.

In part two, we'll use these metrics to compute your health rating and health forecast. To make this process as simple as possible, I'll guide you through the free edition of the Misaic Business Health Monitor, an online tool that does all the forecasting for you. Once you've gone through the process of getting your initial (baseline) health forecast, you'll find that repeating the process becomes even easier. Next, I will walk you through how to interpret the results of your health forecast using examples of various outcomes. Following the generation of your baseline forecast, we'll walk through the process of simulating various changes to the input metrics in order to identify key areas for business focus. Finally, we'll turn our attention to taking action - discussing several approaches to address underlying conditions or risks that your business may be facing, and how to apply further analytics to ensure you can properly react to your findings.

In most of the chapters you will find tables, charts and images that help to illustrate key concepts. While tables print without challenges, sometimes it is a bit difficult to capture the effect of color charts and images in a black and white print book. Therefore, I have posted each of the images used within at www.survivetheodds.com/book1/graphics/ so you can see full size, color images.

As I mentioned in the preface, I have found that providing strategic guidance without tools to activate recommendations results in a struggle for businesses to optimize success. Therefore, I feel it would be a disservice to have this book merely focus on strategy. Instead, I'm compelled to provide the tactical guidance and tools in order to execute the strategies within. This comes with a price such that parts of the book will be a strategic read, and other parts will feel like your reading a text book. So, be sure to keep a cup of coffee nearby as you read just in case.

If you're not a technical or analytic person, the "text book" like sections may feel a bit harder to follow and possibly overwhelming. Don't worry, I've incorporated many examples to try and simplify the concepts. So, don't give up reading; I promise we will not be into the weeds for extended periods of time. Also, if you're not interested in understanding the tactical parts of the book, the key takeaway will be to understand how the pieces fit together so you can properly support your organization in the quest for proper health monitoring. You can always have someone else focus on becoming experts in the tactical execution.

This book is for more than just startups who are trying to beat the undisputed 5-year failure rates that the majority of small businesses will succumb to. Businesses of all sizes and longevity fail, even those that have been around for decades. While enterprise businesses commonly measure or collect the metrics of the health rating formula individually, many do not use a scoring system to assess the collaborative impact of all of them. Here are some examples of well-known large corporations that have either completely failed or reached a failing point, surviving only through Chapter 11 bankruptcy: General Motors, Chrysler, Circuit City, Montgomery Ward, Blockbuster, Hollywood Video, Delta, Pan Am, Lehman Bros.

Hopefully you get my point. No one is exempt from business failure. Today's success is no indication or guarantee of future success. Business survival is not a right, it is a privilege that must be continuously earned, every day. The health rating that is presented within creates a simplified approach for any business to consume; although its simplicity is especially beneficial for small businesses where analytic experts may not exist.

Furthermore, this book is not just about evaluating the health of your overall business, but is just as easily and valuably applied to each of your business segments, product lines or customer segments. It can be the critical tool used to recognize a failing spoke of your business before it's too late. So, survival in this context is not about company survival, but rather product survival.

While you read through the book, you will find the terms health monitoring, health rating and health forecasting used continuously and sometimes interchangeably. Let me provide some clarity to what I mean by these terms. Health monitoring refers to the general process of understanding the health of your business, including its health rating and forecast. The health rating is the actual score that, for a given point in time, represents the health of the business. The health forecast is a projection of health ratings for a given number of periods into the future. By estimating what the health rating for the company will be in the future, you will be able to take actions today to influence that future health rating.

After completing this book, you will have the knowledge needed to implement a continuous process to evaluate your business health, identify critical focus areas, define actions to correct adversities or leverage opportunities, and then measure the impact of the actions you take. Using the free edition of the Misaic Business Health Monitor, you will be able to easily simulate how changes in any of the health rating input metrics impact the short and long term health of your business. I strongly hope that you not only find this book insightful, but that you implement the strategies presented to give your business the best advantage to achieve sustainable success and *survive the odds*. Now, let's get started...

PART I

GATHERING THE DATA

CHAPTER ONE

CUSTOMER DATA

Depending on the nature of your business and the state of your information systems, getting at your customer information may be the easiest or most difficult part of the health monitoring process. It cannot be emphasized enough that understanding your customers is both fundamental and critical to the survival of your business. While it may be hard to accept it, the reality is that since your customers are your business, by not understanding your customers you essentially don't understand your business. Not understanding customer behavior is one of those health hazards that simply waits to catch up to you - just as if you were to eat a stick of butter for breakfast every day.

This need for a better understanding of customer data has been a key factor in the rapid growth and success of CRM (Customer Relationship Management) systems. While CRM software alone is not enough to ensure success, it is a critical part of information management. CRMs serve as a tool to capture your customer's behavior in ways that can be later used for identification of potential risks through the health monitoring process.

If you already track your customer's behavior, "Well done!" You have a head start. But don't get too comfortable because you'll likely soon recognize that you still have work to do, since you're probably not accessing all the pieces you need to get the most out of your customer information. In fact, many companies' information systems make it very difficult to get at the data beyond the pre-built reports that come with the software. If your systems fall into this category, you may need to supplement your systems or decide that it's time for an upgrade. When making these types of decisions, don't think of it as adding complexity to your business, but instead, trust that you're investing in the success and survival of your company. Even if getting the data out of your systems is difficult, once it's captured you're half way there.

Critical Data Elements

In order to effectively support proper health forecasts, your information systems will, at a minimum, need to be able to collect, compile, report and extract the following elements <u>for each customer</u>:

- How the customer became aware of your company
- Date of customer's first purchase
- Date of each transaction
- Amount of spend for each transaction

These four data elements are the building blocks to derive customer metrics for proper business health forecasting. If you're in a service industry, you'll notice that the last three are standard metrics captured with typical POS (point-of-sale) or order management systems. In fact, I've known many small businesses that track this detail in their spiral notebook, as this information is quite basic. To be clear, I do not consider a Mead notebook a typical or qualified POS system.

However, if you're in a retail environment without a loyalty program, then you're likely missing one or more of these items. That's ok. There are ways to backfill what's missing while you get the proper systems in place to start gathering the needed elements. Just remember that your health rating will be more accurate based on the quality of how you have computed these metrics. You should be continually striving to acquire the best quality metrics to support your health forecast.

Filling Critical Data Voids

It may be the case that your business is missing data to support one or more of the critical customer data metrics. The best way to address the problem is to enhance your systems to collect this information going forward. If you already have a POS system or some other mechanism to capture customer transactions (such as Quick Books), then adjust these systems to begin capturing this content. Keep in mind that collecting the data is only the first step. If getting the information out of the system is too complex, then maybe consider alternative approaches to get this detail going forward (see possible options suggested later in this chapter). In the pages that follow, you'll find ways to fill in the missing information until proper collection systems are in place. I've included the purpose of the metrics, as you may have other ways to get to the answer of the underlying question. Sometimes, the only option is to just take a best guess estimate and refine later.

How the customer became aware of your company

Purpose: This metric is designed to understand how customers are learning about your company. This will be combined with your marketing costs to determine cost of customer acquisition.

Ideally you will possess the knowledge of how all of your customers have heard about your company. If you don't already have this, let's start by attempting to gather this information for each of your customers. A couple of approaches to accomplish this exist as follows:

- Ask each customer the next time they come in and track the response in your POS or other customer tracking system that you've enhanced or implemented.
- Send a survey out to your customers and include this as one of the questions. Be sure to include an option for "don't remember" as many customers simply may not. You can estimate this metric using data from those that do remember; hopefully this represents a high percentage.

Alternatively, you many need to start from scratch and begin collecting this information as part of a new customer POS/tracking system. While this may seem disappointing, you'll be surprised how quickly you can build up enough information to start producing valuable insights. Then with time, the quality of your estimates will improve to reduce your margin of error.

Date of first purchase

Purpose: This metric is designed to help determine the total number of new customers per month.

This information will be difficult for any customer to remember off the top of their head. However, I believe that this challenge is most relevant to the retail environment, as service businesses typically capture this information indirectly as part of the order process. If this is a metric gap, I recommend you simply begin to ask your customer if it is their first visit to your store. If the answer is yes, record that and follow-up by asking how they heard about your business. Now you've just captured the missing previous gap as well. The result is not as ideal as having the knowledge of all your customers, but doing this for 30 days' time should provide a decent estimate to be used later in the health rating.

Date of each transaction

Purpose: This data is used to determine customer purchase cycles and serves as an input to determine overall or long-term value of your customer.

This metric will be almost impossible to try and create from scratch. So, if your systems do not currently contain this, then you can collect data over the next 30 days to estimate the metric that fuels the health rating. Using a quick survey approach to estimate this metric, you could ask your customer how often he/she does business with you. With this sample data you can construct a metric estimate until your full tracking system is in place.

Amount of spend for each transaction

Purpose: The goal here is to understand how much customers are spending on each transaction so that we can compute total customer spend per period. This should include if the customer received a discount or not at time of purchase. (Knowing spend at the transaction level will also help with other analysis as you work to improve your health rating.)

Once again, it will be nearly impossible to reconstruct a history for each customer. The best approach to fill a void here is to estimate this value using the actuals from the next 30 days utilizing a proper customer tracking system. In theory, you could ask customers what their average spend is with your business as part of a survey that's either sent via mail, email, handed out at the time of checkout, or even just part of the checkout process. This could give you a quick estimate of how much your customers are spending on each transaction until you can implement proper tracking.

Personally, I doubt customers would likely remember the details of their transactions to give a reliable estimate of average spend. Most people can't remember what they ate for breakfast...but they could tell you if they had breakfast. Then to ask them to do the math to get you an average...yikes. I might stick with just coming up with your own average and track diligently for the next 30 days and beyond.

Ideal Additional Data Elements

While the four metrics listed previously are all that's required from a customer data perspective to compute a health forecast, there are a few more metrics that will be incredibly valuable to either enhance the quality of the health rating or to support recommended actions/treatments to health conditions. Remember that taking action on what you learn is equally important to ensure survival. These following metrics, collected <u>per customer</u>, will drastically improve the value you get back from customer data:

- Items purchased with each transaction
- Details of promotions/coupons redeemed with each transaction
- Demo/Geographic information (income, age, sex, children, zip code, etc.)
- Communication information (email, phone, address)

With just a few pieces of additional information, you will take your insights to a whole new level. The good news is that the first metric - items purchased with each transaction - should be part of any modern POS system (especially computer based software); however, older "registers" do not typically tie transactions to a particular customer. Many POS systems will also capture promotions/coupons redeemed and customer communication information.

At the same time, many service businesses collect promotion and communication information as part of the order process, regardless of the type of POS system used. As for demographic information, this is typically gathered either by a survey or as part of registration for a loyalty program. Remember that for this information to be most beneficial it needs to be known for each customer transaction as applicable (demographic information does not change with every transaction, but it should be kept up to date, storing history).

Customer and Product Segment Level Metrics

One of the advantages of gathering the additional data elements we just reviewed is the ability to support customer and product segment metrics as part of health monitoring. Certainly you can create a health forecast based on a view of your total business; however, creating metrics specific to customer and/or product segments will help produce a more accurate health rating.

For example, imagine a carpet cleaning company, Carpet Masters, which services both residential and commercial accounts. When you look at the customer metrics for these different product lines, their metrics will be much different. The residential customer might only clean their carpets once or twice a year, whereas commercial accounts may have daily, weekly or bi-weekly service cycles. From a pricing perspective, the cost to clean a 3-bedroom home will be much different than a 10,000 square foot office complex.

Therefore, having specific details on both the types of products customers purchase and how much customers spend on those products becomes very important to enhance the quality of the metrics. One of the benefits of the business health monitoring process described within is that it can assess your total business health either by using metrics constructed using all products and customers, or instead, by aggregating each of the individual product and customer segments metrics (if the data is captured at that level of granularity).

Extending this further, you can monitor the health of just a specific product segment (such as residential vs. commercial carpet cleaning services), customer segment (such as frequent shoppers vs. occasional shoppers), and/or specific divisions of your business (such as stores, regions, etc.) by merely creating specific metrics for those areas of interest. These granular, or very detailed, lower levels of analysis are extremely valuable as you determine appropriate strategies for your business.

Building your analysis based on customer or product segments is a more advanced approach to the health monitoring process, but the recommended approach for all businesses. One thing to be aware of when monitoring at the segment level is that some of the metrics you will have collected will only be relevant at the total business level, or may span multiple segments. The way to manage this complexity is to simply spread such metrics across the segments. Typically, this will be done using a weighted average of segment values. For example, general operating costs to run the business might be spread across multiple segments based on each segments share of revenue generated. This means that segments that produce more revenue will contribute a higher amount towards the operating costs. See the following example:

	Segment Revenue	Share of Total Revenue	Share of $10,000 Operating Costs
Segment 1	$10,000	50%	$5,000
Segment 2	$6,000	30%	$3,000
Segment 3	$4,000	20%	$2,000
Total	**$20,000**		**$10,000**

Revenue is only one approach to use for weighting. You may determine that number of customers per segment is a more appropriate benchmark to determine the weights. To keep things simple, some businesses just spread the costs evenly among all segments and skip any type of weighting.

One final tip when working with costs that span segments is to pull out any costs that can be directly attributed to a customer or product segment first, assigning those only to the relevant segments; then, anything remaining that cannot be clearly allocated gets distributed across the remaining segments. For example, suppose a business segment requires its own warehouse to store supplies or merchandise. In this case, those operating costs should be applied only to that product segment.

System Requirements for Customer Data Collection

Having described the important customer data metrics to collect, now it's time to ensure that proper collection systems are in place within your organization. A brief summary of what's required reveals that what's needed is actually quite simple and elementary. For each transaction, an identification of which customer made the purchase must be included. Additionally, the details of the transaction must include what items were purchased, the date/time of the transaction, and any discounts or promotions used. If your systems can provide this level of detail, your customer data will be complete for purposes of health monitoring. Keep in mind that customer demo/geographic information is also helpful; and your systems would ideally enable you to capture that information as well.

The specific system used to gather this information is going to be personal preference and will vary from business to business. There are many factors in making this decision including: cost, hardware requirements, software simplicity, needs for integration with other business processes, etc. For purposes of performing the health monitoring described in this book, the system you choose is immaterial so long as it captures the required information (preferably it includes the "ideal additional elements") AND it allows for you to easily get to the metrics required to compute your health rating on an ongoing basis.

While the ability to export to Microsoft Excel is not a mandatory requirement, typically if your system can export all of your content to Excel, you should be able to compute the required metrics relatively easily. And, if the data is "messy" when it comes out, there are services online such as oDesk (www.odesk.com) where you can hire someone to setup your data for you for a relatively low cost. Done right, you could pay someone one time to build an Excel template that can be reused each month to prepare your data to feed into the Misaic Business Health Monitor.

Another option would be to export the data into a flat data file, often called an ASCII file. Output options such as .csv, .tab, .txt are common examples of such flat files. (Note: .csv files are a common format which can be easily imported into Excel; this is different than directly outputting to an Excel .xls/.xlsx format as mentioned prior.) Once you have data in a flat data file, you can load it into an analysis tool of choice, whether that be a database, Excel or more advanced statistical software. There are many free tools in these spaces to consider; I have a personal liking for MySQL (open source database) and R (statistical analysis software package).

It is a common practice for small businesses to track information in QuickBooks. Depending on how you've configured your QuickBooks software, this may be a viable approach to collect the data. Getting access to the metrics described required may be a bit cumbersome, but if the data is collected, you can usually get there one way or another.

Where to Start

Unless you own a software company, one of the last topics of interest for you to talk about is probably software; especially if you're not technically inclined. I can't tell you how many business leaders don't even know how their software works. On the flip side, there are some leaders that actually know their systems better than anyone else in the company. No matter which side of the spectrum you're on, it's going to be critical for you to either get engaged, or get someone from your company to engage in a proper evaluation.

The first step forward will be to assess how your existing systems support the customer data information requirements outlined in this section. If you are already capturing all the necessary information, then you need to assess how you can get to that information. What reports or data export features are available so you can access and analyze this data? Once you have identified the answer to these two critical pieces, you may have everything you need already in place to begin your health monitoring.

If you're like many companies that find they have some of the information required but not all of it, then you'll need to determine whether or not your software can be enhanced or configured to fill the missing gaps. Assuming you can make the appropriate changes, then begin collecting the full set of information as soon as possible.

If you're in the situation that you do not have the systems in place to collect what you need and your current systems cannot be enhanced to capture everything required, then it's time to search out either replacement or complimentary software. Replacement software means finding an entirely new software package that meets the core business needs that have been supported to date by current software, but also meets the needs to support customer analytics.

Depending on the complexity of your business, this can be very easy or very hard, and can range in the costs required. Some of the most significant challenges you will face with doing a complete migration to another software platform or provider will be transferring your data, changing your business process, and learning new technology. When considering this, evaluate how long you've been using your current solution. Is it clearly outdated? Are there challenges you've been facing anyway that maybe new software could resolve? How much have you invested in this software and what cancellation costs might you incur? What effort will be required to train users, not just on new features but everything they already knew how to do? These are all important factors to consider when evaluating a switch to something new.

If replacing your current software does not seem viable, the alternative approach is to go with complimentary software. This would be an additional software package to support your health monitoring without removing your current software. Since you're going to be modifying your business processes anyway to integrate complimentary software, look to capture all the necessary information for customer analytics, just as in the case of replacement software.

There are two main approaches to implementing complimentary software. The first is to build your own software to fill data voids; which may be particularly viable if you already have a development team. The downside to using your own team is that they likely have critical company projects that could be impacted by having them shift focus. In place of your own development team, you may be able to hire 3rd party programmers to customize something for you.

The alternative approach is to purchase 3rd party software that can fill the voids. Your software requirements to fill these data voids might be pretty unique, so there may not be much available in the off the shelf software market that can provide what you're looking for. If you're not sure where to start, Misaic has affordable software already designed to capture critical health monitoring metrics, and of course, can easily integrate with the Misaic Business Health Monitor software discussed throughout this book.

Whichever path you choose, the critical success factor and action you need to take is to begin capturing the right customer data. The earlier you start collecting this information, the faster you can start using the most accurate information for monitoring the health of your business.

Collecting information about your customers is critical to understanding the health of your business. While several approaches exist to capture this information, commit to take immediate action and ensure you are gathering the basic four customer data metrics required to fuel proper health monitoring. Until your systems are fully in place, there will be ways to estimate the metrics required for your health rating so you can begin monitoring immediately. Remember, the best health forecasts are derived from the most accurate and reliable information, but some estimate is better than no estimate, as long as it is generated using real data. Some people might argue with this statement saying not to use what might be inaccurate data. However, a brilliant PhD statistician once said to me "Even if the statistical significance of the estimate is low or statistically insignificant, it's the only data, thus the best data available, so use it". I like to think of it this way, imagine you have no choice but to drive a car either blindfolded or with kaleidoscope glasses on, which would you choose? While neither is ideal, I'll take the kaleidoscope glasses, you can have the blindfold.

CHAPTER TWO

LOYALTY FRAMEWORKS

Any system that meets the requirements to capture customer transaction details as described in chapter one will suffice for supporting the business health monitoring process. However, there is one methodology that will be the most powerful and direct; and that is to implement software and processes that have a loyalty framework. This means either implementing a loyalty program or utilizing software and processes that would support a loyalty program, hence implementing a loyalty framework.

What's the difference between a loyalty program and a loyalty framework? The difference is in implementation. Loyalty programs are implementations of a loyalty framework, such that customers are aware that they belong to a company's loyalty program and therefore, they expect some type of benefit from being part of the program. These benefits could range from special offers and promotions, special pricing on products, or even earning points redeemable for merchandise. Companies offer these benefits in exchange for being able to use this detailed customer purchase behavior to produce what I consider advanced customer analytics. The insights generated from these analytics are then used to design specialized promotions and offers intended to influence a specific customer's purchase behavior. Companies will typically use a variety of direct to customer marketing techniques including direct mail, email, text messaging, etc. to communicate these specialized promotions. This process was illustrated in the retailer direct marketing to the pregnant teenager example in the introduction.

A loyalty framework simply means having all the customer purchase information to generate the advanced customer analytics as described above, but without having to necessarily promote a loyalty program to the customer. This allows companies to reap most of the benefits of collecting customer purchase behavior without the overhead of a loyalty program. How to implement a loyalty framework without a customer facing loyalty program will be described a bit later in the chapter.

Loyalty Programs

Loyalty programs, done properly and considered "true" loyalty programs, are specifically designed to track the purchase behavior of each of your customers. Loyalty programs can come in many different forms. Some programs have actual loyalty cards (which can be costly and a management nightmare), some use digital mechanisms such as QR codes to identify customers, and others operate by simply using customer phone numbers. Regardless of how the customer presents their membership, true loyalty programs will enable you to understand everything you need to know about your customer to make analytic based business decisions.

Be aware that there are pseudo loyalty programs that have been marketed to businesses which are sold in to be loyalty programs, but are not really loyalty programs. An example of these are punch card programs. You've probably seen these before where you get a stamp, or your card is punched, each time you make a purchase at the retailer. Then after you've filled the card, you get something free or a discount off your next purchase. This may be a viable promotional technique, but it IS NOT a loyalty program. There is nothing about these marketing programs that inherently tracks customer behavior or builds loyalty. The argument is that people will shop there to gain another stamp or punch. If so, they're really shopping there to get a discount/coupon on a future purchase, which is ultimately another form of a coupon. This does not necessarily change customer behavior or promote cross purchasing in the short or long term. In fact, just like any other coupon, businesses may be just rewarding customers for purchases that would have happened anyway. This is not to imply you should necessarily stop programs like this that you may already have in place. It's simply to clarify that these are not loyalty programs; or to avoid semantics, at minimum these do not enable the value of advanced customer analytics.

If you have experience with or are using punch cards or similar type programs, you may have experienced some resistance or disagreement with that statement. So, let's define what advanced customer analytics is all about based on my vast experience building insights and platforms to support customer loyalty analytic solutions for some of the largest retailers in the U.S. The purpose of advanced customer analytics is to understand how customers shop and what influences their behavior, with the intent to modify that behavior for the long-term gain.

For example, if a customer shops in a store once every 2 months, an objective might be to get them shopping once a month. Or, if a customer is already shopping in the store once a month, the goal may be to increase their average monthly spend by 10%. Discounts and coupons may be a marketing mechanism to try and influence these changes, but it is merely a tool to achieve a specific business target/objective; the coupon itself is not the objective. Many times changing this behavior occurs not by discounting current behavior, but rather by getting customers to try new items or services, expanding your product reach to that client. Punch cards on their own do not enable you to track and monitor how you may be changing any individual's purchase behavior, which is at the heart of advanced customer analytics and the purpose of true loyalty programs.

Let me share an example of the right way to do this...Starbuck's. I have no personal knowledge how they're using customer information to promote, but I have some theories based on how good their marketing and offers are and my knowledge of the customer analytics space. I'm a regular Starbuck's customer earning my stars for a free drink after every 12 purchases - conceptually the same as a punch card. But I don't go there to earn another star, that's just a nice benefit. In fact, I've had several free drinks expire because I simply forgot to use them. Instead, I go there because I like their product.

Now, I typically only go there once a day in the morning. In the summer they do a "treat receipt" program where if you purchase a drink in the am, then after 2pm you can get a second drink for only $2. If you were to look at my purchase behavior, my odds of a second purchase in a day must increase 10 fold due to the treat receipt as I often redeem these promotions.

At the same time, other than my free Birthday drink, I don't really get that many drink offers. But I will get offers for food items regularly, as I believe these come to me since I do not typically purchase anything but coffee. Promoting the food items is an attempt to change my purchase behavior, just as the 2pm treat receipt does; and it occasionally works. So, what happens is that the benefits of using my loyalty card to earn stars gives them the knowledge that the treat receipts change my purchase behavior, enabling them to suck even more money from my paycheck, and validate that their promotions work. The cost of a free coffee every 12th drink is worth the value of knowing how well promotions work and how to change customer behavior. This is how you gain value from advanced customer analytics, which as I mentioned before is a topic for an entire book of its own. So let's get out of the rabbit hole and back to capturing customer transaction details.

The good news is that many of the order management or POS systems used by small businesses have the functionality already built in to support a loyalty framework or even loyalty program. That is, they capture all required information to generate advanced customer analytics, and may even include marketing capabilities to execute direct to customer promotions to support the loyalty program. Where most systems fall short is in the generation of the actual advanced customer analytics and insights to design the appropriate targeted marketing promotions, as well as the ability to measure the actual impact of marketing activities. But for purposes of health monitoring, that's ok. If you have the customer data basics, you can at least derive the metrics to support your health forecast. However, being able to produce advanced customer analytics is going to allow you to be much more effective and efficient as you work to improve your overall business health.

Loyalty Frameworks and Cardless Loyalty Programs

At this point you might be asking, "How do I get customer data without a loyalty program?" The answer to this may be a bit easier than you think. First, if you have a service business, it should be a no brainer. Anytime you perform a service, it's expected that the customer will have to give their name. Make sure that when you get the customer's name, gather as much other information as you can including any demographic information they are willing to share. A new customer registration form could be a non-confrontational way to solicit their information. If you can at least capture the customer's name, cell phone, zip code and email, you will have a significant set of what you need to know. This customer information, along with a detailed breakdown of the service transaction, and your analytic power becomes massive.

Online retail is likely even easier than a service business to capture this content since collecting a name and phone number is part of the order process; and the mere nature of being online implies that the order details have been captured electronically. The area that tends to become a bit trickier relates to brick and mortar retail businesses.

So, let's focus on a retail store that sells merchandise through walk-in customers (this includes food establishments as well). The typical scenario is that the customer walks in, selects the product of interest, pays and then leaves. There's no exchange of names, emails, etc. But, why not? There's nothing wrong with asking a customer for their name and phone number. In fact, many major retailer loyalty programs ask for the customer's phone number as part of the checkout process or loyalty program. Some examples include Best Buy, PetCo, Comp USA, Walgreens, Babies 'R Us, Dick's Sporting Goods, to name a few.

In fact, I recently was shopping at a major retailer and as part of the checkout process they handed me a slip of paper with the associates name, the date, some store location information and one blank line and said: "We're updating our records so could you please fill out your email". The funny part was that they do not have a loyalty program and I do not possess their store credit card, so there's nothing for them to update in regards to me. I've never given them this information. But, did I hesitate...no. I gave them one of my many email addresses and went on my way. I'm anticipating that I'll start receiving coupons from them, which I'm fine with since I like to shop there. My guess is that associates are rewarded for collecting completed slips - which would be good process design.

But what if someone doesn't want to give this information? Chances are most customers will provide their number without a blink of an eye. But, you can sweeten the deal a bit by including a rewards program, and therefore explain that their phone number will allow them to accrue points and get special offers. If your software is designed right, it can even provide customers coupons, intended to influence specific targeted behavior as described in the focus of advanced customer analytics, at the register or via text/email. This simple step of providing your customers a recognizable benefit through these offers transforms your loyalty framework into a low cost, cardless loyalty program.

If your company is not up for a rewards program and having to manage customer promotions, that's ok too. You can indicate that the number is used to ensure customer satisfaction and/or is required to lookup their transaction in the case of a return. Or, one of the more recent benefits I've seen offered is the ability to email receipts. This works well for me as I'll go out of my way to avoid having paper piled up on my desk. Think creatively about ways to entice users that may be reserved about providing their information.

In the end, if you can find a way to understand the purchase behavior for just 60-80% of your customers, you will achieve significant milestones in business health and overall growth. But, instituting a "true" loyalty program if you don't already have one is highly recommended. Not only will this fuel the critical data you need to monitor your business health, you will also be able to adjust more rapidly and grow faster by leveraging direct to consumer marketing and measuring the impact through advanced customer analytics.

There are many options out there to help you enter the loyalty space. Be sure that the service you choose allows you to track the actual spend for each customer. Many programs on the market offer really slick technology, but in the end, they really only focus on marketing offers and promotions to customers and/or tracking customer visits to your store; which in isolation is not enough. These types of programs fail to capture what the customer is buying or how much they are actually spending as the customer transacts business. These are two critical pieces of information to support your long-term survival, and therefore these critical elements are included in tracking systems provided by Misaic. Regardless of what software you use, there's never a doubt that the more data you can get, the better off you'll be.

CHAPTER THREE

CUSTOMER ACQUISITION

The concept of customer acquisition and how it relates to the health of your business should be quite obvious. In order for your business to survive and grow, you must always be generating new customers. Does this mean that your business cannot achieve short-term sustainability if it only has a few, or even just one client? Not necessarily. If your single client continues to spend enough monthly to meet your financial obligations, then you can survive - but the risk to your business becomes very high. Once that client switches suppliers or goes out of business, your entire business shuts down. Therefore, not having an ongoing stream of customers is a risk to the health of your business.

Strong customer acquisition is not only about staying in business, but it also leads to organizational stability and sustainable growth. Your business will typically experience some degree of customer loss (attrition), so you must generate new customers as fast as or faster than you lose them. We'll discuss more about attrition in chapter four, but for now, simply acknowledge that attaining new customers is important to long-term sustainability and growth.

Now that we've established the importance of securing new customers, we'll spend the remainder of this chapter digging deeper into the three critical customer acquisition metrics that fuel the health rating formula: customer acquisition rate, customer acquisition cost and customer acquisition variance. With the proper data collection systems in place as described in chapter one, along with standard cost tracking practices, these metrics should be relatively easy to compute.

Customer Acquisition Rate

The first metric of importance is your <u>customer acquisition rate</u>. This is the rate at which you are generating new customers. This can be expressed one of two ways:

Customer Acquisition (velocity) = number of new customers

Or,

Customer Acquisition (% customer growth) = # of new customers /
previous period total customers

It's often easiest to use the former, velocity; as identifying the total number of new customers is typically straight forward. The most simple and direct way to identify velocity is to report the total number of new customers generated in a period. Depending on how your data systems are structured, you may have a field that stores the date of the customer's first transaction, or you may have a report or query that pulls the first transaction for each customer. In either case, you can simply count the number of new customers for that period. Once you have your acquisition velocity, you can simply divide velocity by the total customers from the previous period to determine your % customer growth.

To demonstrate how simple it is to compute your customer acquisition rate, let's revert back to Carpet Masters. See the example below illustrating how % customer growth is derived:

Current Period	New Customers Acquired (velocity)	Previous Month Total Customers	New Customers Acquired (% Customer Growth)
January	10	160	10/160= 6.25%
February	12	170	12/170= 7%
March	13	182	13/182= 7.1%

One of the questions you may be asking is 'How do I determine whether to use velocity or % customer growth for my metric?' The answer will depend on which of the following scenarios best represents your business. If your customer acquisition tends to be relatively consistent as to the number of new customers acquired each period, regardless of how many total customers you have, then velocity is likely the appropriate choice. However, if the number of new customers acquired tends to be growing as your customer base grows, a common case if you have a strong referral program, then % customer growth may be more appropriate. Another way to answer the question is which of the two variations is more consistent or stable.

In the limited data for Carpet Masters above, I might lean towards using acquisition rate, as it appears that velocity is continuously increasing with potentially more variability than % customer growth. However, I would continuously monitor this due to the low number of observations.

It's important to break out your customer acquisition rate by product or customer segment, as there could be different growth rates for each group. Many times companies grow by adding new products to their portfolio; and while their business may be growing, there may be product segments where the number of customers is actually declining. So even if total number of customers is growing, there could be areas of the business experiencing a health decline.

A More Detailed Approach to Customer Acquisition Rate

If you have collected how customers have been sourced to your business, you can take a more detailed approach to calculating customer acquisition rate, creating acquisition metrics for each period for each of the marketing sources. While this may seem a bit tedious, it is extremely powerful. Having the data at the detailed level achieves three important things.

1. By spending the time to collect the best data available, you help to support the most accurate metrics possible.
2. This approach allows you to track which marketing sources are improving or declining over time, enabling you to take very specific corrective action.
3. By having metrics at the granular level, you can simulate the long term impact to the business should any of these sources change. This helps reveal the greatest points of risk in your business so you can work to address them

before they become a significant problem. (Remember in our real estate example that Bob had the majority of his customers coming from one source; which while he may have known that, this forces one to see such risks at every monitoring cycle.)

Considering Carpet Masters again, let's suppose January customer acquisitions came as a result of the following marketing sources:

Source	Customers Generated
Marketing 1	2
Marketing 2	4
Referrals	3
No Marketing	1
Total	10

In the example above, we can not only see that 10 customers were generated in January, but also which marketing activities, if any, were the source of the new customers. Having this level of detail provides a much clearer story relating to new customers.

Customer Acquisition Cost

The second metric of importance is your customer acquisition cost. This represents how much it costs to obtain a customer as determined by the source for which the customer was obtained.

One approach to compute this metric is to simply lump all your marketing expenses together and divide by total new customers generated. Unfortunately, doing that will not provide very informative information on which you could take action.

To make a meaningful impact on your customer acquisition costs, your data system needs to store how each customer heard of your company. This also means that somewhere in the process of managing the customer's first transaction, the system captures that detail. Once you know how each customer was generated, you can simply divide the cost of a particular marketing/sales activity by the total number of customers it generated to obtain your customer acquisition cost (from that marketing/sales activity) as follows:

Customer Acquisition Cost = cost of marketing activity /
number of customers generated

Knowing the costs and customers generated for each marketing activity, you can compute your total customer acquisition cost by summing the costs of all activities and then dividing by the sum of customers generated from each activity, including customers generated without marketing. While we are simply lumping everything together as first described, now you have the critical details needed to make impactful change.

Continuing with our Carpet Masters example, let's add in the costs to the January summary as seen below:

Source	Cost	Customers Generated	Customer Acquisition cost
Marketing 1	250	2	125
Marketing 2	1200	4	300
Referrals	0	3	0
No Marketing	0	1	0
Total	1450	10	145

By having the details at the marketing activity level, we can now see which activities provide the lowest customer acquisition cost as well as identify if certain activities cost more to acquire the customer than a customer is even worth. In particular, looking at the table above, even though marketing event 1 produced less customers, it had a lower cost per customer – suggesting that Carpet Masters should focus more on those type of activities.

While the example above is quite simple, determining acquisition cost per customer is a bit more challenging than one might think. The reason this becomes difficult is because calculating the specific cost associated with marketing to a particular set of customers can be a moving target. Let's explore this further.

For simplicity, assume that your company used only one internet campaign for a two-week duration beginning March 1st. At the end of the month, you identified that 10 new customers came from that internet campaign which cost $100. The math here is really easy, equating to an acquisition cost of $10 ($100/10) per customer. Seems pretty simple.

Now, as you go to compute your customer acquisition cost for April, behold, you find that you generated 6 new customers from the March internet ad. Now, what this really means is that your $100 investment generated 16 customers, translating to a customer acquisition cost of $6.25 instead of $10 which we calculated previously. So here we see our metric for a single activity is changing over time.

How do we overcome this dilemma? The recommended approach is to estimate the life cycle of an advertisement and then allocate the costs to each period according to an estimated decay function. A decay function is the rate at which the impact of an advertisement or promotion declines. For example, most television advertisements have the greatest impact in the first few days or weeks of airing. Eventually, people forget what they saw and the advertisement is no longer generating financial return (we'll ignore concepts of long-term branding).

Let's assume that 80% of the responses to your internet ad will occur in the first 30 days and the remaining 20% will respond in the following 30 days. Based on this, you would allocate 80% of the marketing cost to the first 30 days and 20% to the next 30 days. There are a lot more advanced ways to look at decays, half-life, adstock, etc., but for purposes of this discussion, we'll keep the example as simple as possible to still be effective.

Determining the decay period may seem intimidating at first; but if you have already run the same type of marketing before, you should be able to use previous data to estimate this function. Assuming you've collected how your customers were sourced, simply look at how many customers were generated in each 1-month period of time. Divide the total number of customers generated in each period by the total number of customers generated by the marketing activity, and the result will be your decay function. (Again, this is another opportunity where a bit of data modeling can improve your decay estimates.) Here's an example of computing a decay function from a previous marketing activity:

Month	Customers Generated	Decay %
1	30	66.6%
2	10	22.2%
3	5	11.1%
Total Customers	45	

If you're running a new marketing activity for a given period, it may be best to use the average decay across all your activities to generate your decay function; or if there's a group of activities that are similar, use an average of those.

While decay functions are not exciting by any means, hopefully you can see that they can be simple to compute. I assure you, using simple decay functions like this will help you greatly in the health forecasting process. Thanks for hanging in there.

Customer Acquisition Variance

The third metric to derive is <u>customer acquisition variance</u>. Before I describe this metric it might be a good time to pause for a sip of that coffee, as this may be the most technically complicated section of the book. As we discussed customer acquisition cost, it was identified that there's a complexity in computing acquisition costs when the marketing activity extends across reporting periods. The solution to this challenge was to use a decay function to pre-define the costs to be allocated for future periods.

However, this technique makes an assumption that the exact cost for activity will be covered over the pre-defined time periods (per the decay function), no more and no less. The reality is that there will almost always be some variance to what we forecast to take place, so it's necessary to account for those variances. The way to determine these variances is by using the number of customers generated in the first period as the baseline to forecast future periods, and then adjusting the variance in acquisition costs for future periods. This is best explained via an illustration:

Current Period	March
Marketing activity cost	$2,000
Marketing start date	March 1
Decay (month 1)	80%
Decay (month 2)	20%
Costs allocated for Month 1 (March)	$1,600

Cost allocated for Month 2 (April)	$400
Customers generated (in March)	40
Total projected customers based on March results = 40/.80	50
Projected customers generated in April (20% of total projected customers)	10
Acquisition Cost per Customer ($1600/40)	$40

Based on the table above, you can see that the marketing activity started in March is expected to generate some degree of response through April. Using the estimated decay function, we can distribute the costs of the marketing over both March and April.

Next, using the actual number of customers generated in March, we can estimate the number of new customers in April. This is done by simply estimating the total number of customers expected based on March results, 40 divided by 80%, which equals 50. Next, we multiply that by the percentage of customers expected in month 2, or April in this case, which is 20%. The result of this equation (40/.80)*.20 gives us an expected 10 customers.

Now, let's assume that April concludes as follows:

Period	April
Cost allocated for April (from March marketing)	$400
Customers generated (from March marketing)	8
Projected customers generated in April (20% of total based on decay function)	10
Assumed Acquisition Cost per Customer	$40
April Customer Acquisition Costs	$320
Acquisition Cost Variance	$80

As we can see from the April actuals, we did not generate as many customers from the March marketing as we had anticipated. However, at this point we have allocated all the costs of the marketing event. [Note, our assumption is that the acquisition cost per customer remains consistent from period to period.] Using our acquisition cost per customer of $40, and multiplying by the actual number of April customers, 8, we can get our actual April Customer Acquisition Cost which yields $320. You can see this is different than our expected cost of $400. Therefore, we will cover the $80 difference as part of Acquisition Cost Variance.

At this point, we can create an adjusted acquisition cost per customer metric for the March marketing activity. To do this we simply add up the total customers generated and divide by the total cost. In this case, we generated 48 customers off of the $2,000 investment equaling $41.66. This can now be used to guide future estimates for acquisition cost per customer for this type of marketing activity.

What may still occur is an additional residual effect, meaning more customers are generated beyond April. In these cases, we create a new adjusted acquisition cost per customer, again dividing total cost for the activity by the total number of customers generated. We then create an acquisition cost for the period, defined as *adjusted acquisition cost* x *customers generated,* and then a negative customer acquisition cost variance of the same value to offset the acquisition costs. Continuing with our example:

Period	May
Cost allocated for May (from March marketing)	$0
Customers generated (from March marketing)	4
Projected customers generated in May (decay ended in April)	0
Adjusted Acquisition Cost per Customer (with May results)	$38.46
May Customer Acquisition Costs	$153.85
Acquisition Cost Variance	-$153.85

What we see in this last table is that we have customer acquisition costs for May as we did get four additional customers as a result of the March marketing activity. Since we already accounted for all the costs of the marketing event in April and March (per the decay function), we need to subtract those costs numbers from our total costs for the month because we technically got these four customers for free this month (the marketing event was already paid for). However, we do not want to ignore that in reality these four customers did have a cost to acquire them, so it leads to us doing a bit of numerical gymnastics to make sure that the accounting balances correctly.

So there you have it, the most complicated discussion topic in the book. I may have lost you many paragraphs ago, if so that's ok. The good news is that when using the Misaic Business Health Monitor you will find that acquisition cost variance is an optional input metric for forecasting. However, if you're intending to track your business' health rating on an ongoing basis, it's critical to include this metric to ensure your business' health rating is computed accurately and your trending is correct. This would be a good section to pass off to someone who enjoys the mathematics if you don't.

Non-Trackable Marketing Activities

There's one more complexity to marketing activities that we must discuss before moving forward. In the previous section, we assumed that we knew how many customers were generated by an activity. What happens if you have a marketing activity that cannot be tracked to a customer? This is actually a common situation for businesses.

The ideal solution for this type of scenario is to find a way to measure the impact of these marketing activities. For example, if you've run a radio advertisement, asking your customers how they heard of your company might be all that's required to uncover the value of the radio activity. Alternatively, you could include a special promotion code in the advertisement to entice customers to mention the advertisement upon their visit.

If no compelling tracking mechanism can be created, then you could use statistical models to identify the impact or lift from such advertisements. While such models are not simple to construct, done right, these models can identify the impact of marketing activities and allow you to generate a customer acquisition cost. I've put you through enough mathematical complexities for this chapter, so we won't go into details on such models.

If you are not going to measure these marketing activities either directly or through modeling, the next recommendation I reluctantly give is to lump these costs into operating costs. Why operating costs and not marketing costs? If you add these into your overall marketing costs you could be completely overstating your costs to acquire customers. If you cannot identify specifically that an activity is generating customers, then you should not include it in customer acquisition cost. At the same time, if you are in belief that the marketing activity is needed, even though you cannot prove it, then you should just consider it a cost of operating the business.

With this said, if you cannot measure the impact of a marketing activity, I would suggest you stop doing it. In fact, if you stop the marketing activity and it was providing significant value, then the identification of its value will become much more apparent.

Non-Marketing Types of Acquisition Costs

While we have discussed marketing driven costs, there are other costs to acquire customers that we need to include as well. One of the biggest to consider is the cost of a sales representative. If you operate a call center or have a sales team, you may decide to simply divide the total monthly cost of the call center/sales team by the total number of new customers generated. If you have a direct sales representative model, then you might use the cost of the sales rep divided by number of customers to compute customer acquisition costs. This results in the generation of customer acquisition costs by sales rep, similar to the way described for marketing activities. This will also help you identify performance differences between your sales reps.

If you have a tracking system that defines the actual number of hours invested by a sales rep per customer, this will allow you to even understand acquisition cost differences for each customer; identifying if certain types of customer/product segments (or even marketing activities) result in significantly different sales costs. Whatever your sales operating model, be sure to generate an objective, repeatable way of measuring the costs of your sales team.

Another item to consider in the equation is the cost for general sales collateral/materials such as online sales tools, print materials, order forms, etc. Anything that does not necessarily generate the customer but aids in the sales process should be taken into account. As a result, many companies end up very surprised at how much it actually costs them to acquire a new customer. Until you take the time to assess all the elements, you're just flying blind.

One final point before we leave non-marketing acquisition costs, if a sales representative is needed to generate a sale with a previous customer, I would count that customer to have an acquisition cost as well. If customers are not automatically coming back to your business to purchase without intervention from your sales team, then those customers may not be too much different than a truly new customer, they just might be an easier sell for the representative. As such, it may be valuable to create a separate segment for "renewal customers".

The Manufacturing Paradigm

If you're a manufacturer of goods, you may find yourself in a slightly different marketing paradigm. Many manufacturers have two different sets of customers, retailers and consumers. From a sales perspective, you are typically selling to the retailer, hoping that they purchase your products to put on their shelves. From a marketing perspective, you are designing products for the end consumer who ultimately purchases your products from the retailer. If your company does not do any direct to consumer marketing, then for purposes of acquisition costs you can simply focus on your retail customers to compute the necessary metrics.

However, it may be the case that you also market your products using general advertising to try and build consumer demand for your product, increasing your ability to sell in your product to retailers. In this case, I would still focus on your retail customers as the inputs to acquisition cost per customer; using the costs to build the retailer relationship as the definition of acquisition cost per customer. Then, costs to drive consumer demand can be incorporated into operating costs discussed later in the book. While there is not a hard and fast rule for this paradigm, this should give you some direction on how to think about acquisition costs for this type of situation.

Putting the Pieces Together

Now that we've determined the elements of acquisition cost, let's see how they fit together. For any given period, knowing how many new customers were generated and how much it cost to acquire each (on average), we can now compute our total customer acquisition cost by the following equation:

Total Customer Acquisition Costs = *number of customers*
X customer acquisition cost

For purposes of using the Misaic Business Health Monitor software you only need to derive the input metrics as we discussed in this chapter, however, the Total Customer Acquisition Costs formula is a critical concept to understand when running a business.

This formula is applicable for any historical time period, but can also be used to forecast future values. For example, if we want to estimate how much to expect in customer acquisition costs for next month, simply estimate how many new customers we expect to get and multiply that by the expected acquisition cost per customer, which will likely be based on the historical acquisition costs per customer. The customer acquisition costs formula and application can even be extended to each specific product and customer segment.

In the end, the goal is to try and understand how much it costs to acquire your customers. I know many of my clients have asked me "Should I spend $X on [advertising opportunity]". My first response back to them is "I don't know, what is the long term value of your customer?" This typically results in a long pause, with a gaze like a deer in headlights, and finally a response back to me of "I don't know." You see, the answer can be really simple. If your costs of acquisition exceed the long term value of your customer, then the answer is clearly "No". If the long term value of your customer is greater than the acquisition, then there are other factors to consider, but there's a starting point. In any case, you must understand both your customer acquisition cost and the long term value of your customer. This leads us to chapter four.

CHAPTER FOUR

CUSTOMER REVENUE

One of the most focused on metrics within any business, if not the biggest focal point, is revenue. While there are exceptions, primarily in the case of not-for-profit organizations, the general goal for business owners and leaders is to generate revenue. Revenue is a very important metric as it validates that there is a marketplace demand for the products or services that the organization provides. This should not get confused with the idea that the marketplace necessarily prefers your company over another perpetually; but rather, for the respective period, demand for these types of products and services existed and a certain percentage of the market selected your business to fulfill their needs.

Notice that the title of this chapter is not Revenue, but rather Customer Revenue. There is a very clear reason. When assessing the health of your business, looking at total revenue is not adequate. Total revenue does not give a clear picture of what is happening behind the scenes, including hidden conditions that pose a risk to the business. Thinking back to Bob the real estate agent, remember that total revenue for his business appeared just fine, and in fact nearly identical to that of Susan's. However, in just three months his revenue ceased. Bob was using current revenue as a predictor of future revenue, which was a faulty assumption. This is one example of why understanding *customer revenue* is so important.

Before we get into computing customer revenue, let me first explain what is exactly meant by customer revenue. When I use the term customer revenue, I'm implying the sum of direct revenue from each of the relevant customer/product segments. The actual number that results will typically not be any different than the total direct revenue number reported on the monthly financial statement.

So what's the difference? The difference is in the assumption that in order to compute the customer revenue number, the revenue for each customer group was determined and then aggregated together to get to total customer revenue. Said differently, the key difference is the focus on customer/product groups versus just a total number. Saying that you know your customer revenue is meant to imply that you understand the decomposition of your revenue by customer/product segments and have produced metrics that properly support the health rating formula.

Generating the Customer Revenue Metric

As described above, customer revenue is built from the ground up looking at each of your customer and product segments. It enables you to understand how your revenue is decomposed or dispersed across customer and product segments. Looking at these lower levels of granularity with each monthly review will provide insights to the underlying conditions of your business. It also supports creating health ratings for your customer/product segments in addition to your total business. The formula to compute customer revenue is defined as follows:

Customer Revenue = *expected (direct) revenue per customer*
X *number of customers*

Throughout the rest of the book, unless I specify otherwise, I use the term revenue to imply direct revenue. We'll discuss shortly what is meant by direct revenue.

The part of this equation that is probably a bit different than what you may have anticipated is the use of the qualifier *expected.* The expected revenue per customer can simply be thought of as the average revenue per customer, but it's not necessarily always the average as this is just one way to generate an expected value. There are a few things that could suggest using a different number than the average, which mainly apply when looking at future customer revenue.

First, using data modeling techniques, it may be found that the average may not best represent the expected revenue. In fact, there are various modeling techniques that are designed to get the most probable (or expected) metric which very often is not equal to the average. Second, you may know that something is going to significantly change for a given future period, so the average is no longer appropriate. For example, suppose next month, the price of all services will go up 5%. Then clearly, the expected revenue per customer will not be the same as the average based on the previous time periods.

Expected revenue per customer can be computed at the total business level, or for each of the business's customer/product segments. For a given period, you can reverse engineer the equation to calculate your expected segment revenue per customer as follows:

Expected Segment Revenue per Customer = t*otal segment revenue /*
number of segment customers

By breaking revenue down into its parts, you now can identify if revenue in a period is up or down because of the number of customers or the amount of revenue received from each customer. These are two critical components of the health rating formula.

Let's review an illustration of computing the customer revenue metrics by customer segment. Going back to Carpet Masters, consider March results for their residential and commercial product segments as follows:

	March Revenue	# of Customers	Avg. Revenue Per Customer
Commercial	26,500	10	2,650
Residential	9,000	30	300
Total Revenue	35,500	40	887.50

From the example above, we can clearly see that the revenue per customer is significantly different based on which segment of the business we are looking at, commercial vs. residential. While for some of our later simulation exercises using the overall total revenue per customer may be useful to forecast top level growth, we really should be focused on each customer/product segment.

Direct Revenue vs. Gross Revenue

When computing your customer revenue metric, it is important that you use what I call direct revenue (more commonly referred to as gross profit) and not gross revenue. Let me describe the difference between gross revenue and direct revenue. Gross revenue represents the total amount received for the purchase of the items. It does not account for the cost of the goods sold, discounts, refunds, direct costs, etc. By direct revenue I'm referring to the remaining revenue from the sale of an item after subtracting the direct costs (fixed and variable) to deliver the product, but before deducting any general overhead expenses.

Let's look at an example using a custom t-shirt business, Custom T's, to illustrate the difference between gross revenue and direct revenue. Assume the sale of one of Custom T's custom t-shirts to a customer looks as follows:

Sales Price	$25
Gross Revenue	**$25**
Original Cost of Shirt	-$10
Labor (to customize the shirt)	-$5
Direct Revenue	**$10**

In this example, Custom T's collects $25 for the sale of a customer t-shirt which will account towards total company gross revenue. However, there are certain costs directly related to selling a shirt, including paying someone for 30 minutes time to spray paint a picture on the shirt, as well as the original cost of the shirt itself. Therefore, this only leaves $10 after the sale of the shirt to contribute to general operating expenses of the company. If Custom T's sells 100 shirts with $10 direct revenue each, then $1,000 would be remaining to support the general costs/overhead to run the business. Be aware that any discounts that may have been applied (coupons, etc.) should be deducted before reaching direct revenue metric.

The reason it's important to use direct revenue is that it better represents the impact to the business. For example, if customers shift their $25 of spend to a product that results in only $5 of direct revenue instead of $10, the company health will begin to decline even though gross revenue remains consistent at $25 per transaction. Similarly, if costs of a given product go up, you will see direct revenue decline even though gross revenue remains constant. Another impact could be the need to offer promotions/discounts to maintain gross revenue numbers. All of these are important conditions to understand which cannot be seen by using gross revenue.

Calculating Direct Revenue

Depending on the complexity of your business and/or the sophistication of your information systems, calculating direct revenue may be a little difficult. If your customers typically purchase a single item per transaction, and the costs of that item are known, getting direct revenue can be quite simple. Or, even if multiple items are purchased at a time, but costs for each item are constant and you have a record of each item purchased, then getting to direct revenue again is quite easy. You simply subtract the cost from each item, then sum the items per transaction together as in the following example:

	Sales Price	Cost	Direct Revenue
Product A	10.00	3.00	7.00
Product B	9.00	4.00	5.00
Product C	12.00	5.00	7.00
Basket Total	31.00	12.00	19.00

In this example, the costs are very easy to track and lead to an easy calculation of direct revenue. However, your product offering may have a more complex cost of goods model. If this is the case, look for ways to develop a reasonable model to estimate the cost of goods sold. This could mean using best guess estimates, or possibly creating a few samples where costs are tracked as best as possible and then used to produce an average for the product line.

Let's use Green Machine Lawn Services as an example, where the products offered include lawn mowing, trimming and weed extraction. All three of these services have an element of labor time which can vary, even for similarly sized yards. For example, the number of weeds present will impact how long it will take for weed extraction. The presence of a patio on the property can increase the time to trim. Mowing may be a bit longer if there are hills (in case of push mowers) vs. flat land. However, Green Machine pricing is based on the size of the yard; for example, $25 per mow for a 1/4 acre lot.

Additionally, measuring the exact amount of gas used in the mower and/or trimmer on a given property may be difficult. In this case, it may make more sense for Green Machine to create an average based on servicing several properties, looking at how many properties can be serviced on a single tank of gas. Note, there's another complexity that gas prices fluctuate, so it may make the most sense to measure number of gallons used per property and then compute estimated costs each week based on current gas prices.

Despite how easy or complex it may be to track your direct costs, it's important to focus on creating as accurate measures as possible. There are many ways to track such costs in order to fuel the health rating and options to simplify complex cost models. Invest the appropriate amount of time to ensure you have a model that is fairly accurate, can be replicated ongoing, and can easily adjust for changes to the cost structure. And if you have a structure where estimation is required, be sure to do regular validations that your estimates are still correct.

Why Revenue Alone is Not Enough

Knowing your customer revenue metrics at the granular level provides great insight beyond just fueling the health rating. It provides identification of critical health risks to your business. Let's go back to Carpet Masters and consider the following performance results:

	March Revenue	# of Customers	Revenue Per Customer
Commercial	26,500	10	2,650
Residential	9,000	30	300
Total Revenue	35,500	40	887.50

	April Revenue	# of Customers	Revenue Per Customer
Commercial	21,500	8	2,687.50
Residential	14,000	46	304.35
Total Revenue	35,500	54	657.40

What we're able to observe comparing March and April numbers is that if we only look at total revenue, business appears to be consistent. However, looking into the details we can see the picture is not as rosy. The business actually lost two important commercial accounts that generated $5,000 per month. The impact of these losses was offset in April by the increases sales from the residential side. April is always a high performing month for the residential side as consumers spend their tax refunds doing home improvement work, including carpet cleaning. This accounted for almost all of the 50%+ residential growth in April. This is not sustainable and the business will likely drop back to about 30 residential customers per month come May. Furthermore, while commercial accounts provide significantly more revenue, they are much more difficult to acquire than residential. Therefore, Carpet

Masters' business health is at significant risk for May and beyond as the fundamentals of the business have shifted.

The point of the illustration above is that even though total revenue would suggest the business is doing just fine, the more granular details prove otherwise. Computing revenue per customer at the total business level would have at least identified that there has been a significant change, dropping to $657.40 per customer from $887.50. This could at least prompt an investigation into the cause for the change and then further strategies could be developed to mitigate the risks. This demonstration of alternative perceptions of performance is why I suggest the criticality of focusing on customer revenue, not just revenue.

Customer Purchase Cycle

Another metric that will be important to health monitoring is the understanding of your customer purchase cycle. The customer purchase cycle represents the period of time that will typically lapse between a customer's purchase of your goods and/or services. The purchase cycle will certainly vary by industry, and likely even by customer or product segment. For example, Carpet Masters might find the purchase cycle for residential customers to be every 6 months, while a commercial customer cycle is weekly. Another comparison is gym memberships which typically renew monthly, while auto purchases might be closer to 3-5 years or more.

Why is it important to know your customer purchase cycle? Knowing customer purchase cycle metrics will allow you to better estimate how much revenue to expect in a future period. Back to our carpet cleaning example, if Carpet Masters has a customer base of 120 customers with a typical purchase cycle of 3 months, then they could estimate the expected monthly customers as 120/3 = 40 customers per month. Extending that further, for any month they could estimate the revenue to be 40 customers x $300 (the expected revenue per customer) = $12,000.

The customer purchase cycle will be important to understand as you look at your health forecast, as a purchase cycle greater than the reporting period span (typically one month) will mean that you may have more fluctuation in numbers between cycle times, but over the course of one purchase cycle, things should average out. For example, maybe the 40 customers per month do not spread out evenly over the 3 months, but rather might distribute as 35, 55 and 30; still totaling 120 for a three month period.

Another value in knowing your purchase cycle is to compare it to industry standard metrics to identify if you have a risk to your business (as purchase cycles start expanding) or opportunity with your customers to improve purchase cycles. For example, the industry recommended oil change is every 3 months (depending on your vehicle and oil choice). In a perfect world, an oil change shop should see its customer purchase cycle equal 3 months. If instead its purchase cycle is 5 or 6 months, it could indicate that customers are splitting their oil changes between companies; or it may identify an opportunity to increase revenue from customers by getting them to complete their oil changes more regularly.

Gaining Additional Value from Customer Revenue Metrics

Having customer health metrics at the granular level will certainly support the needs for health monitoring, but it will also provide some important insights into your business for better decision making. Remember the common question that I get from business owners about spending on advertising..."Should I invest $X in [advertising activity]". With the metrics we just defined, we can start to answer this question with a bit more confidence.

Let's say that the expected revenue per customer is $300 and the advertisement in question costs $150, then the question now becomes "Do I think I can generate at least one customer from this marketing activity?" If the advertisement costs $1200, then the question translates into "Do I think I can generate four customers to break even or obtain 1-3 customers and keep them for at least 2-3 purchase cycles?" While there are still more points to consider in the decision process, hopefully you can begin to see how to make more informed decisions by having granular customer metrics. We will see the analysis for this question improve even further as we incorporate attrition rates in the next chapter.

If you're not currently tracking direct customer revenue by segment, you're not alone. I've found this to be a common gap not only in small businesses, but large corporations as well. You'd be surprised how many large companies don't actually know if their product lines are profitable. It's a systemic problem. As a company grows, even though the number of employee's grows, so does the amount of work that needs to get done. As a result, proper monitoring typically remains neglected and a critical gap.

Focusing on total revenue alone is not sufficient to assess the health of your business. It is imperative that you expand your focus to include direct customer revenue. Furthermore, analyzing customer revenue at the customer/product segment level will help you better understand the dynamics of the business, as well as produce the most relevant customer revenue metrics. Combining expected revenue per customer with purchase cycle information, you can begin to build foundations for forecasting revenue. Let's move on to the final customer metric for the health rating equation...customer attrition.

CHAPTER FIVE

CUSTOMER ATTRITION

One of the biggest opportunities to improve your business health is through focus on customer attrition. While everyone is familiar with the idea that it costs 6-7 times more to acquire a new customer than it does to retain a customer, it's surprising that many businesses do not focus more on customer retention and attrition.

However, there are some large organizations that demonstrate a best practice and heavy focus on attrition. In fact, you'll find these companies have setup special "customer retention departments" where customers are routed to upon calling in to cancel their services. These departments are empowered to make special provisions for the customer in order to retain their business. Cellular phone companies illustrate this model well. However, it's much easier for them to allow for provisions as a cellular phone company knows the long term value of the customer, since the service is a monthly subscription for a fixed term.

There's more value to gain from controlling attrition than just the cost savings vs. acquiring a new customer. Attrition can provide an indicator that there is potentially something fundamentally wrong with your business, which could impact many of the previous metrics we've already covered.

For example, if customers are defecting to go to a new competitor that has opened up in the area, you should expect that your number of new customers per month may start declining. In addition to stealing customers, your competitor may be offering lower pricing and thus force you to do the same, driving down your average revenue per customer. Attrition could also be a result of bad customer experiences. This could result in reduction in referrals, decreasing new customers and potentially leading to further attrition problems.

Attrition may not only slow or stagnate your growth, it could actually lead to company failure if or when your attrition rate exceeds your customer acquisition rate. This concept is really simple, if you lose more customers monthly than you generate, eventually you will not have enough customers to support running the business. While there may be several reasons that customers are defecting, it is critically important to not only understand the metric, but also the causes.

Calculating Customer Attrition

Let's start by explicitly defining what customer attrition means for purposes of the health rating formula. Customer attrition is simply the loss of customers from your business and is also referred to as customer churn, customer turnover or customer defection. For the health formula, we consider two possible views of <u>customer attrition rate</u>. The first is the actual number of customers lost, or otherwise attrition velocity:

Customer Attrition (velocity) = *number of customers lost*

However, we will sometimes consider the attrition rate to be expressed as a % of total customers:

Customer Attrition (% customer attrition) = *number of customers lost / previous period total customers*

The use of attrition rate becomes especially useful when considering simulation exercises. In some cases, you may expect the number of defectors to be constant. However, the reality is that as a business grows, so will the number of defectors, such that attrition rate might be fairly consistent (without intervention) and can be a better metric to estimate the attrition for a future period.

While the definition of attrition is simple, how do you go about identifying lost customers? If your business operates in a subscription model, models where customers register for continued services (fitness clubs, athletic programs, online services, etc.), then lost customers should be quite easy to determine as you simply look at the number of cancellations for the period. If a customer is purchasing multiple services, then they must cancel all services to be considered lost, as they would otherwise still remain a customer of the company with a reduced set of services.

However, if you are in a business model where customers choose to do business with you at their will, then we can use purchase cycles to help determine when a customer is lost. The simplest method is to look at a typical/expected purchase cycle for the product class, and then define an appropriate number of missed purchased cycles to determine that a customer has defected. I recommend a default of two purchase cycles, without knowing the details of the product class.

For example, consider the oil change business mentioned previously, if a customer has not returned within 6 months (expected purchase cycle is 3 months), then it could be fair to assume that they have defected. This simple method of computing attrition can work well, especially if most of your customers make purchases within 2 purchase cycles.

A more advanced method to determine attrition is to use various purchase cycles that are relevant to customer segments. In this approach, your customers are segmented based on their purchase frequency. Then, each customer is determined to have defected if they exceed 2 purchase cycles within the length defined by the segment they belong to. This is especially important if purchase cycles can vary widely across customer groups.

For example, suppose Carpet Masters commercial business has been segmented into three customer segments with the following purchase cycles:

Segment	Purchase/Service Cycle
Premiere	Daily
Frequent	Weekly
Occasional	Monthly

The final approach that we'll discuss is to model the purchase cycle for each customer. In this methodology, you are able to determine more accurate estimates of attrition. When applying this more granular approach, you may choose to incorporate probability models to determine the right purchase cycle length to use in considering the customer lost. For example, a particular customer may have a 50% probability to purchase in one purchase cycle, a 60% probability to purchase in two purchase cycles, and an 80% probability to purchase in three purchase cycles. For this customer, it may be more appropriate to use three purchase cycles as the trigger to consider the customer lost. There are other advanced techniques you can consider as this was just an example of the power of using advanced models to improve your attrition metrics.

Given the importance and impact that attrition has to your business, I encourage you to seek out ways to maximize the accuracy of your attrition metrics. With that said, do not avoid starting with the simplest approach while you work towards more advanced methods, especially if developing advanced methods will create significant delays. It's better to have a simple estimate than no estimate. Remember...kaleidoscope glasses are better than a blindfold.

Lapsing

We're going to diverge from metrics that fuel the health formula for a moment to discuss a concept called lapsing. While lapsing is not a metric that's required for the health rating, it's closely related to attrition and therefore it's worth a short discussion. Lapsing occurs when a customer does not make a purchase during a typical purchase cycle. Let it be clear that the definition of lapsed has mixed meanings in the marketing world. I would not get as caught up in the semantics as it is the concept presented within that is important to understand.

As we relate this to attrition, it is very similar. However, the key difference is that a customer that has lapsed is not necessarily a lost customer as many marketers may be quick to define. It just means they did not make a purchase within the normal purchase cycle. Lapsing is a very important metric as it can be a way to identify potential attrition before it happens. For example, let's say the normal purchase cycle for Customer X is 2 months. If after 2 months since his last purchase, Customer X has not returned for another purchase, we would consider him lapsed. Now, if we use the default of 2 purchase cycles as the criteria to define lost, then after 4 months of no purchase activity Customer X would be considered lost. In between 2 and 4 months of no activity, we would consider Customer X to have lapsed.

Since we've already gone through the effort to determine the appropriate purchase cycle for a customer, whether that be the industry standard, segment average, or customer modeled, it only makes sense to leverage that purchase cycle estimate to identify lapsed customers on a per period basis. Knowing which customers have lapsed provides you the opportunity to communicate with them before they have a chance to defect permanently. There are many ways in which you can choose to communicate including but not limited to social media, email, direct mailer, text messaging, coupons or even direct phone call.

Looking at lapsed customers is another area where advanced analytics can come into play, determining the probability of a customer lapsing based on previous behavior so that you know where to place your customer retention efforts. Another step further would be to identify the characteristics that lead to customer defection, delving into the realms of predictive analytics. All of this begins to fall into discussions of advanced customer analytics and customer centered marketing, both of which fall outside the scope of this book. The important take away here is that purchase cycle information can be leveraged to attack potential attrition problems through identification of lapsed customers.

Attrition by Segments

Now that we've defined attrition at the total business level, we can extend the concept to customer/product segments just like the previous metrics we've discussed. Going back to Carpet Masters, it may be valuable to understand how commercial customers are defecting vs. residential customers. It may be that the commercial side of the business is at risk due to new competition that is not competing with the residential business.

To evaluate attrition at the product segment level, it requires us to modify our definition of lost customers. We previously stated that a customer is lost when he/she is no longer purchasing any services from our business. If we're evaluating customer segments, this definition does not change as customers should only belong to one particular customer segment. So, if a customer within a segment has no purchases, he will be considered lost. However, if we are evaluating product segments, then we will consider a customer lost if they are no longer purchasing within that product class, even though they still may be a customer of the business.

Imagine a customer who hires Carpet Masters to perform cleaning services for her residential home. Upon satisfaction with the services, the customer decides to extend the services to her business cleaning needs as well. In this case, the customer is spanning two different product segments, residential and commercial. If she decides to cancel her commercial services but maintains her residential service, then she is considered a lost customer to the commercial business, even though she is still a Carpet Master customer for residential services.

Being able to distinguish attrition metrics by segment is extremely important in managing the overall health of your business. If one product segment is gaining customers as fast as another segment is losing customers, then when only looking at the total business view, everything will appear satisfactory. However, there's an underlying condition in the business that suggests that a product segment is declining. Let's review the following illustration:

	Previous Period Customers	New Customers	Lost Customers	Net Customers
Product A	100	5	15	90
Product B	60	20	3	77
Total	160	25	18	167

In the above example we can see that from a total customer basis the company appears to be improving, seeing an increase from 160 to 167 customers, about a 5% increase. However, Product A customer base is declining, dropping from 100 customers to 90 and representing a 10% decline. If Product B is a replacement for Product A, then this change may not be bad from a business perspective. For example, if Product B is a product upgrade producing higher direct revenue, then shifting of sales from Product A to Product B is ok. On the other hand, if Product A and B are independent of one another, then clearly business growth will be diminished by the decline of Product A.

While there's tremendous value to assess the health of your business at the total business level, it can be just as important to perform assessments at the segment level. The example shown above was a product segment example, but the impact and importance is just the same for customer segments. Identifying attrition problems at the segment level enables tactical decision making to prevent business decline and/or maximize business growth. Since the principles of lapsing discussed previously apply just the same at the segment level, you can get ahead of a more serious attrition problem within product or customer segments.

Understanding Causes of Customer Attrition

Before we move off of the topic of attrition, I feel it's worthwhile to discuss the importance of understanding the causes of attrition. First, we must distinguish that there's a difference between natural attrition and elective attrition. Either type of attrition is un-healthy as it will lower the health rating of your business. However, natural attrition does not necessarily reflect a negative condition of your business.

Natural attrition is likely to exist in any business environment and is not reflective of the quality of the services provided, nor a result of competitive activity. Natural attrition occurs when consumers no longer are in the marketplace for the products or services that your company provides.

For example, consumers might move out of the area and thus, can no longer can be serviced by you or your competitors. Or maybe the product or services that you provide have a known lifespan, such as child care, orthodontics, education, bankruptcy services, etc. These all are only relevant for a specific period of time for a given customer.

An area where natural attrition, as well as defining the rules for considering a customer defected, becomes a little more gray is with products that have a long purchase cycle such as autos, real estate, travel services, etc. In these cases, it is plausible to retain a customer for life, but the purchase cycles are so long (3, 5, 7 years apart) that it's difficult to identify if a customer is lapsing or if they have forgotten about your company altogether. This is why many companies in these industries strive to maintain regular contact with customers.

Businesses in such industries can find great benefit in segmenting their customers as they may find individuals that move frequently, buy new cars every year or two, or travel multiple times per year; each of these examples provide significant deviance from the typical purchase cycles. It is very common to have some segments where attrition is expected upon the completion of a transaction, while others may in fact have an opportunity for lifelong relationships.

Elective attrition occurs when customers elect not to continue services with your company but remain in the market for your goods and services, and as such, these customers have typically selected another provider. This type of attrition is the most concerning and needs to be carefully understood as it may represent business conditions that can lead to long term decline and possible failure. While there may be many causes of elective attrition, most can be classified into these five categories:

Pricing: Customers are able to find the same products, or substitutable products, at a lower price through a competitor. The internet has had a huge influence on this condition.

Convenience: Customers are able to find the same products, or substitutable products, through a location that is more convenient. This does not necessarily mean that the other provider is necessarily cheaper as people will often pay a price for convenience. Again, online shopping has also been a contributor to this phenomenon.

Product Differentiation: Customers are able to find more preferable products elsewhere. These could be either better quality of similar products, products that better meet the client needs, or even a broader selection of additional products to simplify their shopping to one supplier.

Dissatisfaction: Customers are dissatisfied with the products or service experience at your company. While dissatisfaction is a poor way to lose customers, extreme satisfaction through excellent customer service and strong relationships can often overcome the other five categories of attrition. Therefore, focus on customer satisfaction should be a top priority in every business.

<u>Social Influence</u>: Customers are lured to another competitor by referral from their social network. Alternatively, it could be that customers are inclined to leave your company due to a negative experience at your company from someone they know, even though their experiences may have been adequate.

It is critical to understand these causes of attrition and their applicability in your attrition numbers, as each has a different set of actions to help mitigate or improve the condition. While computing the attrition number will help you see the macro view and impact to the business, understanding the causes will enable you to improve and influence attrition metrics going forward. There's an added benefit that by understanding the factors of attrition, mitigation strategies can not only reduce attrition, but may lead to higher customer satisfaction among non-defecting customers and even influence a higher revenue per customer metric.

Even if you are in alignment that understanding the cause of attrition is important, you may be wondering how to identify the cause. This indeed is the tricky part. There are quantitative and qualitative ways to get the answer.

The best way to understand the causes is to measure it quantitatively through direct and indirect surveys. For example, setting up a process to survey your defected customers to ask the reason they left is going to provide the most accurate and direct answer to the cause. This would be a direct method to quantitative measures. It may be difficult to get responses from all your defected customers, but an investment in the effort will pay back huge dividends from the learnings. You could try automated ways to reach the client such as email, direct mail, or even text surveys; however, do not hesitate to use direct phone calls as the primary approach, or at minimum the last option if no response is received from other methods.

The indirect quantitative approach is to do regular surveys of your current customers to infer the possible drivers of attrition. If your surveys are not anonymous, you may even be able to identify possible causes for defectors based on recent responses. For example, if your survey identifies that a customer felt the value for your products may be low and then they defected, you could make a reasonable inference as to why they left. This type of data mining becomes even more powerful if you have patterns in the data that identify similar behavior across customers.

The alternative approach, or additional method to support quantitative research, is to use qualitative research of the marketplace. For example, you may notice trends happening with competitors entering or leaving the market. You can use social media to identify what people are saying about your company or your competitors. While this approach will be much more speculative in nature than actually asking customers directly, this can be a powerful way to compliment other research.

None of these approaches needs to be done in isolation. In fact, I encourage you to apply all three. Survey your defected customers to understand the real reason behind their defection, survey your current customers to identify problems before the customer decides to defect, and stay abreast of changes in the marketplace so you can be aware of external impacts to the business, allowing you to adjust accordingly.

Determining the Long Term Value of Your Customer

Now that you have an understanding of attrition within your business, you can determine the long term value of your customer. Again, this is not a metric that's required for the health forecasting, but an important concept for business success; so I can't help but take a tangent here to provide some guidance.

There are actually many different ways to determine the long term value of your customer; in fact, enough to dedicate an entire book to the topic. However, I want to give you at least one way to compute this metric for your business. If you've followed the process of collecting the customer information to support the attrition metric, we can use this detail to identify how long a customer will typically remain a customer of your business.

For this approach, determine a fixed time period to qualify as the "long term". This could be as long as your company has been in business; however, I find it more common to use between a 2 and 5 year fixed term for a variety of reasons. In any case, this approach will require that you have the data to support the customer metrics that we've discussed; going back as far as the length of your defined term, or possibly even a few periods beyond.

Now, we first need to determine your average customer lifespan – not how long they live, but how long they will be a customer of yours. Start with the first period of the term you've defined, and using your new customer acquisition information, identify all new customers for that period. For example, if you're using a 36 month (3 year) term, identify all new customers acquired 36 months ago. In the world of statistics, this group of customers is what we would call a cohort. Now, using your customer attrition data, for each of the customers in this cohort, calculate how many months passed until the customer defected – this will be each customer's "lifespan". For those that are still customers, their lifespan will be equal to 36 months (the length of the set term). Add up all the lifespans calculated from this cohort and divide by the number of customers in the cohort. The result will be your average 36-month customer lifespan.

Before we move on to use the lifespan to determine the long term customer value, it is important to understand a few things about this process. First, if your starting period only has a small number of new customers, this may not be a large enough sample to represent your total business. In this case, you will continue to work backwards from the first period, repeating the process until you get enough customers to have a viable sample.

For example, if there were only 12 new customers generated 36 months ago, then after computing the individual customer lifespans for that cohort, repeat the process for the new customers generated 37 months ago, considering this group the second cohort. Repeat this process until you have enough customers to feel comfortable using the data.

If you need to extend beyond a single cohort to derive your average customer lifespan, then two adjustments need to be made. First, the max individual customer lifespan needs to be set at 36 months (or equivalent to the term you've set). Second, you must add the individual customer lifespans from all cohorts together first, and then divide by the total number of customers in all cohorts combined.

The second call out about this process is that your retention rates may change significantly over time. For example, you may have made significant improvements in your products or services such that more people are likely to stay now than, say, 2 years ago. Or, on the contrary, maybe there's more competition in the area so there's a greater chance that a customer will defect, thus shortening your average customer lifespan. These are just some of the reasons that I recommend a smaller lifespan term for analysis using this type of approach. There are more advanced ways to model average customer lifespan which are beyond the scope of this book.

After you've determined your average customer lifespan, and assuming you've computed expected direct customer revenue as described in the previous chapter, then your long term customer value can be computed as follows:

Long Term Customer Value (LTCV) = expected (direct) customer revenue
X average customer lifespan

Once again, you can create the LTCV metric at the product or customer segment level to provide better quality metrics. Having this general understanding of the long term value of your customers will provide tremendous support in marketing decisions.

Revisiting the common question "Should I invest $X in [advertising activity]?", we now have the most data driven approach to answer the question. At this point, we can simply divide the cost of the advertisement by the long term value of a customer to determine approximately how many customers the activity must generate in order to recoup the investment. There are still other factors to consider, including total time to recoup the investment, other activities that might be more effective, confidence in the how many customers can be generated, etc. However, the confidence in decision making becomes much stronger having customer metrics to support the analysis process.

Attrition, while a simple metric mathematically, has significant influence to the health of your business. This metric can be misleading when evaluated only at the total business level; therefore, it should be accompanied by evaluation at segment levels. This detailed level of analysis will enable you to better manage segments of your business and minimize risk that unhealthy segments get overseen by well performing segments. The good news is that through proper analysis using purchase cycles, lapsing metrics, and customer surveys, attrition levels can be controlled through early detection of negative business conditions. I encourage you to focus heavily on understanding attrition within your business, above and beyond the minimum requirements to support the health rating formula.

CHAPTER SIX

OPERATING COSTS

We're going to move off of customer data and shift our focus to data that your business should already have accessible to support your typical accounting reports...operating costs. Operating costs should be something that every business is already tracking in some form or fashion, as you cannot properly complete your business income tax returns without having the expense side of your business known. However, there are a couple areas of difference that exist between how I define operating costs here versus what you may be familiar with.

Defining Operating Costs

The key difference between operating costs and direct costs discussed earlier is that operating costs exist whether you are running at 100% capacity or 50%. These costs do not typically increase in relation to supporting more or less customers, with the exception of stepwise costs which we'll cover later in the chapter. For purposes of the health rating formula, we will define operating costs as follows:

Operating Costs = *fixed costs to operate the business independent of sales*

Examples include rent, insurance, salaries (for non-sales reps), utilities and wages. Essentially, everything that was not part of the costs used to compute the direct customer revenue metric should fall into operating costs.

Now, traditional accounting practices will include metrics such as interest earned, taxes, depreciation and amortization in the final evaluation of the business financial statement. While depreciation and amortization have a valuable place to assist in taxation rules, we are not going to consider those items here. We will, however, include any interest earned as a reduction in operating costs; unless receiving interest is a product offering of the business, then it should be included as part of customer revenue. We will also add any taxes paid as part of operating expenses as it reduces the cash available to the business; of course tax credits should positively impact operating costs.

With that said, I'm going to propose a new view of looking at costs in the business for which its purpose is purely to support the health evaluation of the business. As I walk through this method, I'm sure to make accountants cringe and by no means should this method be used for purposes of income tax reporting. This does not make the method bad or incorrect in any way, it's merely a different way of thinking.

See, the currently accepted methods of accounting are designed to support the tax laws, and these tax laws were written in the interest of providing income to the government, not for ensuring the future success of a business. This is partially why the view of EBITDA (earnings before interest, taxes, depreciation and amortization) exists, as it provides investors another financial view of a company different than what the IRS is concerned with for taxation purposes. Note, there is some criticism on the use of EBITDA for investors as it may not accurately represent profitability. You won't see me publishing a book on this topic for sure, so feel free to research the subject online if you really want to understand this more. In any case, we need to consider another view of the business that has one objective in mind...providing business leaders with an understanding of the true health of their business without any need to fit into the closed box of IRS rules.

The method of accounting I'm presenting follows a hybrid of the cash and accrual methods of accounting. In this method, we will count income and expenses as earned or incurred based on when they are <u>due</u>. This means even if a customer does not pay you on time, we will assume that payment will occur within a reasonable period of time and still credit that revenue in the period it was due.

For example, suppose you sold a product for $6,000 to a customer to be paid in 12 monthly installments of $500. In this method we will not count the $6,000 sale in the first month, but rather $500 in each monthly period. Unless this was a subscription service, accrual methods of accounting would normally count the $6,000 at the time of the contract. Even if the payments are not received on time for a given month, the revenue will be assumed to be earned in each period rather than when it was actually received as in the case of cash basis accounting (if a subscription).

For expenses, we will see the reverse scenario. If we purchase an item for $6,000, but agree to payments of $500 per month, then we will spread that expense out over the 12 months. This differs from accrual accounting methods where we would normally account for all $6,000 of expense when the purchased item was delivered, regardless of the payments being spread out. This is especially different for items purchased on a credit card, where both cash and accrual methods would count the expense at the time of purchase. Instead, we spread the costs out for each month of credit card repayment. Additionally, if we were late to pay a creditor as part of any installment terms, the cash method of accounting would have the expense hit the books the month it was actually paid rather than due.

You may be wondering "What's the value of adding another type of accounting into the mix?" The main reason is that it is important to identify if the business is able to sustain itself month after month given the revenue expected to be collected versus expenses to be expended. Looking at expenses or income that hit in a given month but represent multiple months of value, impact, or service is misleading. This is not to say that cash flow is not important, in fact, it is quite the contrary. However, the business is apt to show more swings in positive and negative months based on cash flow or accrual accounting methods; but the reality is these large fluctuations are merely an accounting technicality for the given month, and instead, such transactions represent a longer term expense to the business. Said another way, success is about a long term system of profit generation; thus a business is successful when it can consistently produce greater revenue than its expenses.

Inventory Costs

Now it's time for another twist from traditional accounting, which deals with the purchase of inventory or materials to support direct product costs, or costs of goods sold. Remember that we have already accounted for the cost of goods sold in our customer revenue metric. However, we need to account for any upfront costs for inventory or materials to support product sales, as these will occur in advance of the actual sale of the merchandise. At the same time, if we account for the initial spend for inventory in our operating costs at the time it's purchased, then we will end up double counting it later when we compute customer revenue (remember customer revenue subtracts the costs of goods sold from gross revenue). Therefore, as part of operating costs, we are not going to include any costs for inventory or other materials that will be subtracted from gross revenue as part of computing the direct customer revenue metric. We will handle inventory acquisition costs as part of the next chapter, reserves and inventory.

One last element of inventory costs that needs to be addressed surrounds any interest or financing fees resulting from inventory purchases. Since you should receive the principal amount back on the inventory at the time of sale, that part of inventory costs will be recouped. However, suppose that inventory is purchased with financing options, either from the supplier directly, a business loan, or even a credit card. This means each month there will be interest charged on the unpaid balance. Interest will not be recouped and therefore should stand out as its own expense, and I recommend that it be included in operating costs. If your business purchases inventory with cash or 0% financing, then this topic will not apply.

The alternative approach to manage interest expense is to include it into the direct cost of goods sold. I believe this adds more complication than it benefits. One of the challenges is that the total interest will likely not be fixed or known at the start, as it depends on how long it takes you to repay the loan – which may even be subject to changing interest rates. Therefore, it cannot be evenly distributed across the inventory.

Additionally, the interest is not necessarily tied directly to the sale of the merchandise. For example, suppose you financed $30,000 of inventory with the expectation to sell that inventory over the next 6 months. But, in the course of business you were able to generate enough profit to pay off the $30,000 after the first month. Even though the inventory has only depleted by 1/6th, the interest for the month was for all the inventory. You can see in this example that the interest is not directly tied to the sale of the merchandise and the total amount will vary depending on how long it takes to repay the financed principle. If I've confused you just trying to explain the problem to you, all the more reason to just include it in operating costs.

As far as allocating interest expenses for inventory purchases, you can use the approach that makes the most sense for your business. The important strategy to implement is simply not to include the principal costs of inventory purchases as part of your operating costs.

Stepwise Costs

One of the cost elements that often gets overlooked by business leaders is stepwise costs, also known as step costs. These are costs that remain constant but then increase once a certain level of output is reached. The new level is typically constant again until another level of output is reached. The following chart [6.1] illustrates the concept of stepwise costs:

What we can see from the example above is that fixed costs increase as units sold moves from 40 to 50 and then 70 to 80. The first jump is only a small increase while the costs to support 80-100 units is nearly double that of 10-40 units. Reasons for stepwise increases can vary, but could result from a need to increase fixed labor, office or warehouse space, or additional equipment leasing to name a few.

Evaluating the impacts of stepwise costs is often overlooked as businesses forecast future growth. A failure to understand and include stepwise costs can reap havoc on the future success of a business. For example, if a business is striving to reach a certain amount of volume so that revenue can cover expenses, but then shortly after reaching the point of profitability the business grows to a point of hitting the stepwise costs, then the business is back to losing money once again. The result is a business model where only a small set of revenue intervals are actually profitable.

Let me illustrate this by overlaying direct revenue as seen in chart [6.2]:

In the above chart, we can see that the business only operates profitably when selling roughly between 30-45 units and 60-70 units. The important element to identify here is that stepwise costs can create a different financial picture of the business versus specific data points. For example, if the business is operating today at 40 units this will actually be a profitable output point. Many leaders make uninformed decisions and assume that by doubling output from 40 to 80 that profits will also double. However, doubling output in this case would actually lead to negative profits. Therefore, it's important that you be sure to understand stepwise costs that may exist within your business structure, especially as you forecast future growth for the business.

Opportunity Costs of Management

There is one more cost that should be included in the operating costs, and an expense that never hits the accounting books - the foregone cost of salary for an owner's time. The nature of many small businesses is that the owner gets paid after everyone else is paid. If there's no money left over, the owner goes without a paycheck. In some cases, the owner takes a small salary, and then if anything remains at the end of the period, then he/she will take a distribution.

The challenge with either of these approaches is that the business is potentially not paying for a cost that should exist in the business. If a business cannot pay for managerial support, it should be considered unhealthy. At minimum, you should be including the cost for management of the business based on what it would cost to hire someone for that role. This expense should be included in your operating costs even if the payments are not being made.

Now, it's debatable the amount that should be included in operating costs. That is, whether or not the amount should be based on market value for that role or based on the opportunity income for the owner. For example, suppose an individual left a corporate job paying $150k per year to run a pizza restaurant, as that was her dream in life. If the average salary to manage a pizza restaurant is $60k, than at least the $60k expense should be included in operating costs even if it's not being paid out. If the owner needed to step out of management for any reason, then the business would need to hire someone for that role and thus require revenue coming in to support that payment. While some would argue that you should include the $150k salary, this does not make sense as you are adding artificial costs to the business. Meaning, if you were to take over a business that had the manager earning 2.5 times the industry average, the right thing for the business would be to replace that cost with a more reasonable salary.

With that said, we do not have to leave the $90k gap ($150k minus $60k) out of the evaluation of the business health altogether. Instead, we can incorporate this opportunity cost into the reserves metric, which we'll discuss in the next chapter.

Calculating operating costs should be one of the most straightforward metrics to compute as your company should already have the necessary data collected. However, there will be some additional work involved as you translate your current data into the slightly different view of operating costs presented here versus traditional accounting methods. As you go through the process of computing operating costs, be sure not to count inventory costs or any costs of goods sold into the metric; and remember to include any opportunity costs for managerial salaries that may not be getting paid at market value. Thinking ahead to business growth and opportunity, be aware of stepwise costs that can impact the operating costs of the business. Now, let's discuss the last set of metrics for the health rating formula...reserves and inventory.

CHAPTER SEVEN

RESERVES & INVENTORY

The last set of metrics required for the health rating formula should be the easiest to identify and compute. Since the two are closely related, we'll cover both in this chapter. Before we dive into the definition of these metrics, let me explain why these two are closely related and serve as the foundation of the health rating.

The key purpose of creating the health rating is to determine how effective a business is at providing a return on the capital invested. If a business is healthy, then the return on investment will be favorable. On the contrary, a failing business will provide negative return on investment, such that the business continues to eat away at all the capital investment until eventually there's no more cash to keep the business afloat.

The metrics discussed up to this point determine the overall performance of the business and are the key underlying drivers of profit; hence I call these the performance metrics. However, these last two metrics, reserves and inventory, provide the benchmark as to whether the performance of the business is satisfactory given the investment; hence I call these the benchmark metrics. Let's understand the definition of these foundational benchmark metrics.

Defining Reserves

The term reserves might be ambiguous at first, but the definition is quite simple. Generally speaking, we can think of reserves in the following manner:

Reserves = *Capital Investments In - Capital Investments Out*

While this definition probably needs no explanation, I'll spend a moment to avoid any confusion. Upon the start of almost any business, there will need to be a capital infusion. This initial financial investment has in and of itself, an opportunity cost. These dollars are sitting available somewhere, whether in a bank, personal savings, angel investors, or in the hands of shareholders prior to the initial investment. These dollars, for right or wrong, were selected to be used for the chosen investment at the opportunity cost of other investment choices. One of the reasons I use the term reserves rather than capital investment is that it reinforces that these dollars were in fact on reserve for selective use from whichever source or sources supplied them.

The other influence for the use of the term reserves goes back to my experience in real estate investing. In the lending industry, the bank likes to see that you have sufficient reserves available when purchasing an investment property, typically an amount equal to six months of expenses. This helps protect the loan in the event the property goes vacant, as the investor has the ability to pull cash from "reserves" to cover the expenses. Similarly, reserves here represent cash to support any unprofitable state of the business.

In addition to the need for initial investment, often throughout the course of business additional investment is required to expand the business or even just keep it afloat. Again, these dollars come from a reserve somewhere and represent an opportunity cost of those dollars. These additional contributions to the business will also constitute reserves.

Based on this definition, you can determine the value of reserves for a given period as simply the amount of capital investment collected during the period less any repayments of capital investment. This should be a very easy metric to compute. The only additional twist to this metric would be incorporating opportunity costs from the owner as discussed at the end of chapter five. In that example, the owner of the business is foregoing $90k worth of income per year above the standard salary for the role, which equals nearly $8k per month. It would be reasonable to include this into the reserves contribution even though no cash is being physically exchanged. However, this is still an artificial cost to the business and is relevant when the owners are looking to evaluate the proper use of their time and capital.

Defining Inventory

Back in chapter six, we discussed that purchases for inventory should not be counted in operating costs and instead handled as its own entity. When we use the term inventory here, we are including any materials or goods that are directly used to complete a sale, and thus included into the cost of goods sold. The inventory calculation can be defined as follows:

Inventory = *New Inventory Purchased - Inventory Depletion*

Computing inventory is very straightforward as you simply subtract any inventory sold from any new inventory purchased. Let's revisit Custom T's to see how the inventory metric is computed:

	T-Shirt Inventory Acquired	T-shirts Inventory Depleted	Inventory Metric
March	$5,000	$1,200	$3,800
April	$0	$1,000	-$1,000

Typically, inventory will be purchased with cash from within the business. However, sometimes the business may not have the financial ability to purchase inventory, and therefore, an additional cash investment is made or owners purchase the inventory on their personal credit card. In either case, be sure to capture the owner's contribution as additional reserves into the business. Then, only reduce the reserves upon any principal repayments.

For example, if an investor provides additional capital for $5,000 worth of inventory, then reserves will increase by $5,000 and inventory will increase by $5,000. Any interest paid to the investor (or credit card) will be accounted for as part of operating costs. Only principal payments reducing the $5,000 balance will count as a reserve reduction. When inventory sells, it will reduce the inventory number, but will not reduce reserves unless payments are made directly back to the investor.

Setting Initial Reserve and Inventory Values

Since reserves and inventory are used to determine the benchmark for overall health, we must include the cumulative values for both reserves and inventory to enable proper forecasting. When we get to using the Misaic Business Health Monitor later, there will be a metric called Initial Reserves and another for Initial Inventory, the latter being optional in the event inventory is not applicable for your business. Essentially, the value to enter here is the accumulation of all reserve transactions through the prior period. The same would be true for inventory, but inventory can more easily be determined by simply using the current inventory value/level; since this represents the cumulative result of previous inventory changes.

For example, suppose your business opened in January of 2013, and you are planning to forecast starting the current period of May 2013. Then we can determine the Initial Reserves value as represented in the following table:

	Reserves In	Reserves Out	Cumulative Reserves
Jan '13	$50,000	$0	$50,000
Feb '13	$0	$0	$50,000
Mar '13	$10,000	$0	$60,000
Apr '13	$0	$0	$60,000

In this example, we can see that an initial capital infusion came in January to get the business launched, and then another $10,000 was invested in March. Therefore, assuming the current period is May 2013, we would have an Initial Reserve metric of $60,000.

In the absence of having this background of information (maybe this information was never tracked for your business), you could start measuring the health of the business from the current point in time as your benchmark going forward. In this case, you would use reserves as defined in relation to the current available cash in the business as described in the next section.

Alternative Approach to Defining Initial Reserves

Depending on where a business is in its lifecycle, rather than using capital investments to define initial reserves, reserves can alternatively be defined based on current cash available as follows:

Reserves = *total cash available*

In this definition of reserves, we are evaluating the health of a business relative to the current cash available. The purpose for this type of view is to support resetting the health rating based on a given point in time for which initial capital investment is no longer relevant, as the owners have recouped all the initial capital investments; or possibly the capital inputs and outputs are not able to be determined.

In the case of resetting the reserve benchmark based on available cash, the key question for the business owners or leaders is whether to pull cash out of the business to invest elsewhere, leave the cash present to remain as reserves, or to invest the cash in the business to accelerate further growth. It is important to assess the health of the business under each of these scenarios.

Available Cash

After determining your reserves and inventory levels through the current period, you must define your available cash. This is simply the total cash available in the business, represented by cash held in checking or savings accounts; but also includes any other sources of cash (eg. petty cash).

This is a very important metric as it helps to determine how much of your reserves remain, as well as identifies if your business will run short on cash to operate in future months. It also allows the formula to self-correct for any rounding errors or missed items that may have occurred to date while using the performance metrics to determine overall cash position.

While computing reserves and inventory metrics should not be very complicated, these two metrics are critical as they serve as the benchmark for whether or not the performance of the business is ultimately healthy. The eight metrics we have discussed come together to provide a quantitative approach to measuring the health of any business. By setting up the appropriate data collection systems and processes to compute these metrics, your business will be prepared to extract valuable insights towards its future trajectory and thus, enable you to adjust your strategies accordingly. So, with the steps in place to gather the data, let's move on to measuring the health of your business.

PART II

ANALYSIS FOR ACTION

CHAPTER EIGHT

SMOOTHING THE DATA

In Part I of this book, we defined how to compute each of the metrics that will fuel the health rating formula so you can generate a health forecast for your business. Before jumping into applying these metrics, we need to define two possible key objectives of the health rating; and depending on your focus for analysis, you may or may not need to apply data smoothing. If you're unfamiliar with the concept of data smoothing, don't worry, we'll get to the definition in just a moment.

The first objective you may have is to evaluate the business health rating for a specific period, enabling you to identify where tactical plans may have underperformed or exceeded expectations. In this case, using the raw metrics without applying data smoothing may be sufficient.

The second objective would be to monitor how the business is trending or performing on average for the purposes of forecasting, in which case, we would want to smooth the data. In general, for purposes of forecasting, it will typically be more appropriate to use smoothed data vs. the latest period (or any other period); however, exceptions to this rule will exist. It is also a plausible use case to use the raw metrics for the current period and then use the smoothed metrics for forecasted periods.

We'll spend the remainder of this chapter discussing techniques to smooth the data. I want to note that just as before, these data smoothing techniques can apply to product or customer segments. That is, you can create specific smoothed metrics that vary by each segment.

What is Data Smoothing?

While the term data smoothing may sound complicated, it's actually quite simple. Data smoothing is a process to remove the natural variances that will occur from period to period for a given metric. A simple way to smooth the data is to take an average of the metric over time. Using an average of the metric will result in less fluctuation from period to period. In the chart [8.1] below is an example of smoothing a customer acquisition metric:

In the example above, we can see that on a month by month basis the number of new customers can vary quite drastically;

however, using the average tends to produce a more consistent metric. If we were to look at the actual number of new customers, it's quite unclear as to what's happening because of the large amount of variability. However, looking at the average, it shows that the number of new customers appears to be declining.

The downside to using a simple average to smooth the data vs. more advanced modeling techniques is that the actual number from period to period can vary greatly from the average for valid reasons. You can see this type of gap occur between April and August in the previous chart. There are a few simple techniques that you can apply to enhance these estimates, as we'll discuss next.

Seasonality

While taking a simple average will work in many cases, we want to be cautious to not confound seasonality into our averages. Seasonality exists when certain times of the year tend to consistently result in significantly different metric values, whether this be new customers, sales, attrition, operating costs, etc. To give an example of a highly seasonal business, let's consider a college or university where new customers (students) are typically going to be generated on regular enrollment periods. Fall tends to generate higher levels of new student enrollments than spring, and spring contains higher levels of new students than summer. Therefore, each of these periods might be best represented by separate estimated acquisition rates, with at least one other rate of acquisition for enrollments in non-peak periods (just after the semester starts, but before the tail end of the semester).

111

Going back to our previous example, let's suppose that we know that there is a high seasonality for this product creating peak demand in the months of Apr, May, Jun, Nov, Dec and Jan. In this case, we'll want to separate the averages by seasonal periods. This means that rather than just one overall average, we'll actually create two separate averages; one using data from peak season months, and one using data from non-peak months. Let's plot peak season versus non-peak season as shown in the chart [8.2] below:

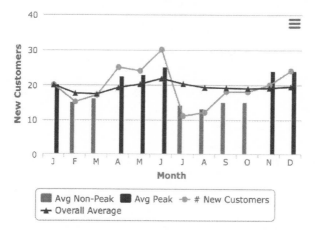

Looking at the revised chart which incorporates seasonality, we can identify a few different outcomes. In order to highlight the separate peak vs. non-peak values, I've displayed them as columns rather than lines. First, notice that the average for each seasonal period (peak and non-peak) is much closer to the actual number of new customers versus using an overall average. This has improved our overall estimation approach, showing much less variability than before.

Second, we can now see that the peak season at the end of the year seems to be on par with the mid-year peak numbers resulting from the average; indicating that we did not necessarily see a decline in our business during peak season, the most critical time for revenue generation. On the other hand, we may have missed some opportunity during the off-peak season as we see a little bit of decline, but the drop does not appear too significant. This is a different story than when we looked at the same data without accounting for seasonality, which suggested that our customer acquisition rate overall was declining.

Moving Averages

Another technique that is helpful in generating smoothed data is the use of moving averages. Unlike the previous examples where all data history was used to generate the average, the moving average only uses a select number of periods to compute the average. Assuming there's no seasonality to control for, a 6 month moving average would use the metrics from the last 6 months to compute the average. This allows you to track how the average is changing just as before, but because there are only 6 data points, the most recent period will have a much larger impact on the resulting average as it represents 1/6th of the data. This allows us to better identify trends that are happening as a result of time.

Review the table below to see how to compute a simple 3-month moving average (MA):

	Sales ($)	Months Used to Compute 3-Month MA	3-Month Moving Average ($)
Jan	5,600	NA	NA
Feb	7,000	NA	NA

	Sales ($)	Months Used to Compute 3-Month MA	3-Month Moving Average ($)
Mar	9,000	Jan, Feb, Mar	7,200
Apr	8,300	Feb, Mar, Apr	8,100

For simplicity, my recommendation is to use either a 3, 6 or 12 month moving average; however, if you're familiar with moving averages you may choose another interval as deemed appropriate. If your data has a lot of variation in the metrics, then a 6 or 12 month moving average might be most appropriate. The one issue with 12 month averages is that you may not be able to capture trending as easily, as the business may be growing or declining over time and it gets lost in the big picture. If you're data has less variance from period to period, the data is likely to be trending up or down, or you are implementing new strategies on a regular basis that may be causing the variation, then a 3 or 6 month moving average might be more appropriate.

You can still use moving averages if you have seasonality to control for. If you're computing an x-month moving average, then when you select your periods, you should include the last x month's values within that seasonality group. For example, in our case of peak seasons earlier, it was identified that peak seasons consisted of January, April, May, June, November and December. If you were to compute a 3 month moving average in November, you would use data from months November, June and May.

By reducing your availability to only 3, 6 or 12 periods of data for purposes of using a moving average, you may have only a few data points for estimating any specific metric. Sometimes this could mean that using this average may not be representative of future events. In the perfect world of statistics, observations have at least 30 data points; however, the goal here is to base decisions off of the best data that you have access to, even if that's only a few data points.

Since many real world business problems do not have 30+ data points, at Misaic, we actually developed a proprietary data estimation model that can create estimates that are more accurate than traditional statistical methods and models; especially when working with a very small number of data points. This method is called MPM (Most Probable Metric) Modeling. Although MPM Modeling prefers to have a minimum of 6 data points, it has proven to produce accurate estimates with as little as 3 data points. This proprietary modeling technique works on almost any metric.

For those looking to increase your health rating estimates, consider modeling the data to produce the best estimates possible; whether this be through MPM Modeling or your own modeling techniques.

Performance vs. Benchmark Metrics

The data smoothing approaches described here can be applied to all the metrics mathematically; however, these may or may not be appropriate for benchmark metrics. If you recall, performance metrics work together to describe how well the business performed from a profit perspective. These metrics will be relevant for each business period.

On the contrary, benchmark metrics, that is inventory and reserves, may or may not change during a given period.

Depending on the type of business you operate, inventory may be a continuous and somewhat consistent metric. If so, then smoothing this metric for forecasting and trend evaluation would make sense. Similarly, if capital investments are continuous in your business, then this too could be smoothed. However, continually adding reserves is a sign of a potentially unhealthy business, since it means you are continuously investing more and more cash into the business as the business cannot support itself. Therefore, I would hope that this is not a situation that your business is facing. In any case, choose to use data smoothing as it best fits the conditions of your business.

There are several approaches to smooth your data to provide the most appropriate metrics for your health rating and forecast. You should almost always use a smoothed metric for forecasted periods. The exception would be in the case when you know the expected value of the metric in the future period, or in the case of simulations where you are setting period targets. When smoothing data remember to control for seasonality and also data trends. While advanced data modeling will provide the best estimates for your metrics, using averages is a valid technique to generate simple, but useful metric estimates. Producing smoothed data by segments will further enhance the quality of your overall metrics and thus ultimately, your health forecast. Now that we've covered getting your data ready, it's time to apply this information to the health rating formula.

CHAPTER NINE

BUSINESS HEALTH FORECASTING

Finally, we're ready to apply the formula that is going to assess the overall health of your business and prepare your organization to make decisions and take action that will promote sustainable success. I developed the health rating formula exclusively for Misaic to enable its customers to achieve sustainable success. Based on the research discussed in the introduction, most businesses do not even generate all the metrics required to fuel the formula. This provides a competitive advantage for those that do implement the health monitoring process and apply tactical strategies to improve their health rating, as you will be able to operate smarter than your competition.

In this chapter we're going to review how to use the free edition of the Misaic Business Health Monitor software so that you can easily compute your health forecast. As a result, this chapter will be a combination of general knowledge as well as a pseudo training guide, which will come in handy when you're actually ready to use the tool. The purpose for including it here, however, is so that you can understand how simple it is to compute your forecast as well as tie together the software with the key knowledge components. Look at that, I may have gone far off the reservation by combining a business book, text book and training guide into one...maybe I should have charged more.

While the Misaic Business Health Monitor takes the mathematics to produce the health rating and forecast out of your hands, you will still need to compute the input metrics to feed into the formula as described in Part I. However, the free edition serves as a simple way to implement health monitoring in your business with the following features:

- Input your critical metric values to generate your business's current health rating
- Create and save your 60 month baseline health forecast, identifying your business's current trajectory and sustainability
- Generate your business equilibrium metrics and identify any additional reserves that may be required to enable survival
- Simulate how changes to your metrics will impact the health forecast (we will cover simulation in chapter eleven)

The Misaic Business Health Monitor has many advanced features beyond the free edition that enhance the monitoring process and focus on improving metric accuracy; these will not be discussed in detail as part of this book. You can learn more about advanced features on the Misaic website at www.misaic.com.

Accessing the Online Tool

The first step to start benefiting from the health monitoring software will be to setup your free account at www.businesshealthmonitor.com. The setup process is simple and should be able to be completed in a few minutes. All you will need is access to the internet and a valid email address. After answering a few questions about your business, your userid and password will be emailed to you. You can then return to the website and login to begin.

Setting Up Your First Forecast

Once you've logged in with your new account, you will be presented with the main health monitoring screen which should look similar to the following illustration [9.1]:

Health Forecast

Status: At Risk

Forecast: Potential for Survival

Ending Period Profit	$ 0
Ending Customers	0

Simulator Off

Break Even — Closure — Health Rating

Update   Settings   Save

Customer Acquisition	Base
# of new customers:	
Acquisition Rate (%)	
Acquisition cost:	
Acquisition cost variance:	

Direct Customer Revenue	
Current number of customers:	
Expected revenue per customer:	

Customer Attrition	
# of lost customers:	
Attrition Rate (%)	

Operating Costs	
Operating costs:	

Reserves and Inventory	
Available cash:	
Reserves:	
Reserve adjustment:	
Inventory:	
Inventory adjustment:	

A few points to note as you initially login. First, the graphic presented above is based on printing of this book. It is expected that over time the software will undergo changes and may look different than depicted above, or possibly may not appear as the first screen after logging in. Second, since this book is printed in black and white, you will not be able to see some of the color coding that is visible when accessing online. Utilize the link provided in the introduction to view these images online. In particular, you will see a green line for 'break even' which is horizontal with a consistent health rating of 10.

Additionally, the values for the customer metrics are all blank since upon first login, you have not saved a default forecast. Therefore, the health rating forecast depicted by the dark gray line is equal to zero for all periods. Finally, the forecast summary box located next to the top right of the chart will reflect an empty forecast as we just described.

The next step is to prepare your forecast by filling in the health formula metrics in the bottom half of the screen. All of the fields should look familiar to you as we discussed them in Part I. You'll see that the acquisition and attrition metrics provide a drop down so you can input velocities or percentages as most appropriate to your situation. Any of the fields in italics are optional fields and are not required to complete the forecast. Once you make a change to any of the metric values, the 'Update' and 'Save' buttons will change from gray to green.

Running Your Forecast

After you've completed all the required (non-italic) fields, you can run your forecast by simply clicking the 'Update' button. After doing so, you will see the chart update and the forecast summary box will refresh. You will also notice that the 'Save' button will remain green, which means that you have not yet saved the changes. Below is an illustration [9.2] of the result of running a forecast:

In this particular example, we can see that the business forecast somewhat resembles the shape of the letter U. While you will not be able to see the color in this book, there is a solid horizontal red line for 'Closure' at Health Rating of 0. Also, on the x-axis you will see the forecast go out to 60 periods, where periods represents months.

Understanding Health Rating Values

While several metrics feed into the health monitoring equation, the overall health of your business is summarized by one number, the business health rating. As you interpret your business health rating for any point in time, a rating of 10 or higher is considered healthy. A rating below 10 is unhealthy and represents that the business has not yet returned back the capital invested. Finally, a value less than or equal to zero represents that the business has gone under as cash has run out.

To explore the health rating a bit further, the higher the health rating, the healthier your company is, as you may have expected. Comparing health ratings from various product/customer segments can be useful to evaluate which business segments are more successful; again, in the sense that they provided a return on the capital invested. If you were to compare health ratings from two different companies, it will tell you which company has a better return based on the capital invested. However, that does not mean a company with a higher health rating has higher revenue or higher profits, as it depends on how much money was invested in each of the companies. Only if the same amount of investment was made into the two companies would the health rating indicate which company outperforms the other.

The Forecast Summary Box

As noted previously, there is a summary box located in the top right of the screen. In this example, there is a tab called 'Baseline' which is the default name for the forecast. In the summary box the system will dynamically populate the status and forecast text that describes the situation, using red (high risk), orange (moderate risk) and green (healthy) colored text to highlight the status. Following the status and forecast, you will find some key metrics about the state of the forecast.

In this example, it is highlighted that the business will need an additional $6,998 of reserves (or capital investment) in order to survive the period of time where the business is below a 0 health rating. Each forecast will also describe the profit level at the end of the period. If the business has reached equilibrium at the end of the 60 periods, then rather than displaying 'Ending Profit' it will display 'Equilibrium Profit'. We'll discuss equilibrium profit later in this chapter.

Finally, we can see the number of customers that the business should have at the end of the forecast period. It's important to validate that the number of customers seems reasonable and can even be supported based on the assumed resource capacity (including human, inventory, operating, and real estate resources).

Saving Your Forecast

After you've made changes to any of your input metrics, the 'Save' button will turn green, indicating that you have not yet saved your changes. You can update the forecast as many times as you'd like, but nothing will be saved until you press the 'Save' button. Upon saving your latest changes, the forecast will run again, in the event you did not update before hitting save, and this will be the new default forecast that runs the next time you login.

In addition to changing your metrics, you can change the name of the baseline forecast in case you want to identify when you created the forecast, or any other short descriptor that has meaning to you. Simply hit the 'Settings' button to bring up the options screen. You will see a box for Forecast Name. Simply rename the forecast as you desire and then hit the 'Save' button.

Business Equilibrium

While developing the health rating formula, one of the observations that became apparent was the concept of business equilibrium. What this means is that if the input metrics to the health rating formula were to remain constant, the business will eventually reach a state of equilibrium, in which the health rating grows at a constant rate; note this can only occur if the health of the business is positive long term. When this happens, monthly net profits reach a constant value, called equilibrium profit; and therefore the business cannot grow any faster without changing the values of the input metrics. You can see this phenomenon occur in the previous chart somewhere around 25 months. At this point in time, the rate of increase of the health rating remains constant; or otherwise said, the slope of the health rating forecast is constant. The chart does not display the equilibrium profit value, but it can be found in the Forecast Summary Box as mentioned earlier. Neither the health rating value nor the point in time equilibrium occurs has influence on the actual equilibrium profit value; as this will be a function of the performance metrics.

Understanding business equilibrium is important for multiple reasons. First, if you are able to achieve business equilibrium, your business has an opportunity to sustain itself. Second, knowing the amount of time it takes to reach equilibrium can provide a sense of how far away your business is from reaching a stable state. Finally, understanding the value of equilibrium profit allows you to assess the monthly net profit and decide if the value is acceptable. If not, then you must positively impact the input metrics. Also, you can compare the equilibrium profit from one business to another, or equilibrium profit by business segment, to decide where your investments should be focused.

Now, business equilibrium is a theoretical concept as it is unlikely that your input metrics are going to remain constant. But, even though metrics will change, identifying business equilibrium will still provide you a rough idea of how long until your business is stable and a gauge of what your monthly profit will be.

Hopefully you've found that producing a health forecast using the Misaic Business Health Monitor is simple, yet powerful. By supplying just a handful of input metrics, the health and trajectory of your business can be described with one simple health rating value. You can use this tool to forecast your business as a whole, or for individual customer or product segments. Now that you have the tools needed at your disposal to produce your health forecast, let's continue on to learn how to interpret the results.

CHAPTER TEN

FORECAST SCENARIOS

At this point, you should be able to compute your input metrics and generate a health forecast for your business, whether using the free edition of the Misaic Business Health Monitor software or an advanced edition. It is important to remember that baseline forecasts represent the health of the business assuming the current input metric values remain constant over the next 60 months. Now, let's discuss various forecast scenarios that may result and how to interpret their meaning.

The Ideal State

Let's begin with what I wish every business's forecast could look like. The following chart [10.1] displays the perfect picture of a healthy business. Now, this does not include any considerations for risky input metrics which we'll discuss later.

127

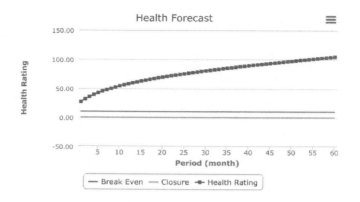

What you'll see in the ideal forecast above is that the business is already starting at a healthy state, with a health rating above 10. Then in less than 3 years, the business reaches equilibrium. Not shown on the graph here, but equilibrium profit is approximately $5,200 per month. Assuming that's an acceptable profit return, this business appears to be a worthwhile and sustainable entity. If the owner has included her managerial salary into the operating costs, then she could leave the business, hiring on a manager, and have a monthly income stream of $5,200 per month. Also, depending on the riskiness of the input metrics, $5,200 appears to be a fair amount of cushion to manage abnormal months so as to not disrupt the long term sustainability of the business.

This type of resulting graph represents a healthy business that has opportunity to thrive and survive. If your business forecast looks similar to this, first of all...congratulations, nicely done! Be careful, however, as it only takes slight changes in the input metrics to alter the shape of the health curve. Therefore, focus closely on input metrics that have a large amount of variability or are already known to negatively change in the future. Also, while the business forecast looks favorable, this does not mean that it is generating the monthly profit that is acceptable to the business leaders. Be sure to assess the equilibrium profit for acceptability and monitor risky conditions that can impact this currently favorable profit stream as we'll discuss in chapters eleven and twelve.

The Successful Startup

By sheer nature, starting a business requires an upfront investment that will be at risk. Therefore, almost any viable business will appear unhealthy in the first part of its lifecycle. This is not to say that the business cannot be profitable very early on, even day one. However, most businesses will require a capital investment for startup expenses including computers, supplies, salaries, phones, internet, rent, etc. Therefore, earning profits early in the life cycle is a great achievement, but that begins the repayment process against the initial investment. The following chart [10.2] shows what a successful startup forecast may look like:

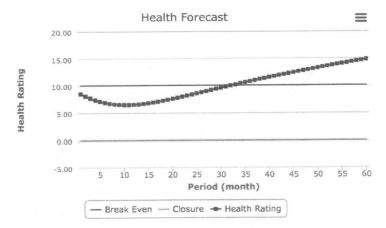

129

Notice that this startup starts off with a declining health rating as it lacks enough business to make a profit. But before the investment is exhausted, it achieves profits (around month 12) and then works its way to a positive health rating in year three. Then, by the end of the third year it approaches equilibrium and continues to become healthier. Less than 50% of businesses that start are able to reach this type of sustainability; that is, making it to the 60th month. Therefore, this would be a great outcome for any starting business.

One of the key risks when experiencing this scenario is the unknowns of the startup period. If your business is truly in startup mode, then some of your input metrics may be based on very few data points and you lack historical data trends to identify seasonality or other external influencers to your business. Also, consumer demand for your products or services can shift dramatically. Hopefully you will actually see demand increase over time, but if your market size is smaller than anticipated, then your acquisition rate may start declining before your company reaches a healthy state.

For example, suppose you open up a new retail shop in a small town. You might see your number of new customers growing fast for the first 6 months as the word spreads about your business. However, soon you will run out of new customers as the population of the town is small and fixed.

While the health rating in the example presented above appears to be quite distant from zero, be sure to carefully and continuously monitor the lowest point of your health rating curve. If your health forecast dips close to zero, you may need to consider planning for additional capital, especially in the event that your input metrics negatively change.

The Typical Startup

Given that less than 50% of startups achieve an outcome demonstrated by the previous graph, this leaves an unfortunately high number of businesses experiencing a forecast similar to the following chart [10.3]:

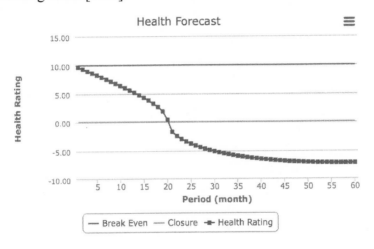

In the typical startup, we see the health of the business start with a decline and then it never comes off of that trajectory; such that at some point in the first few years the business ultimately fails. While the example above shows the failing point around 20 months, the period in which the business actually reaches zero health rating can vary. If your business forecast looks similar to the curve above, you need to take action quickly to change the outlook. We'll look at where to focus in chapter eleven when we discuss simulations.

The Close Call

This next example, which I name the close call, is not too much different of a scenario than the successful startup. I believe that a fair portion of the businesses that shut down, do so because they believe their forecast looks like the typical startup, headed for failure, and they give up. However, little do they know, they were just a handful of periods away from actually surviving. Here's a chart [10.4] of a business whose forecast represents a close call:

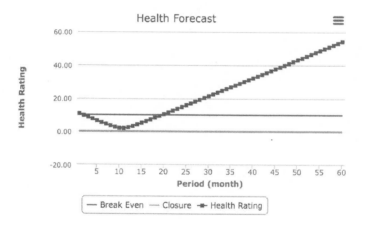

What's incredibly interesting about this example is that nothing has changed in the input metrics. Even though the business appears to be headed toward failure, the natural evolution of customer acquisition along with customer attrition changes the trajectory of the company. Unfortunately, what happens in practice is that many businesses may give up after about a year or so, expecting that they will not survive, when in fact they are actually on path to survive.

Now, with that said, this is a risky situation as any negative deviation in the metrics can result in failure vs. success. This is a case where a sound strategy can change the fate of the business. But, only by having the knowledge from a proper health forecast can the owner truly identify that success is even possible, especially in the eye of what appears to be failure.

If this is the forecast that your business faces, it is important that you become aware of this as early as possible for three reasons. First, knowing early gives you ample time to influence the input metrics so that you can potentially avoid cutting it so close. Second, you can consider infusing additional capital before it's too late to react in time. Finally, knowing that the business has a positive future can help prevent closing the doors prematurely as well as minimize any loss of desire to continue as the business appears to be on a downward spiral.

The Missed Opportunity

Similar to the previous example, there are businesses that are meant for success but never have the opportunity to reach their full potential. In this next chart [10.5], we see a business that is forced to close before it is able to reach its equilibrium state, which in fact yields a long term healthy business:

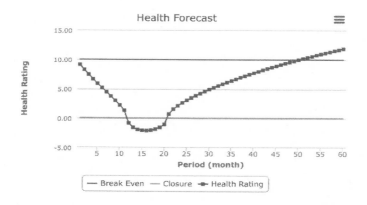

In this example, we can see that the business runs out of capital after 12 months; however, had the business been able to fund itself for another 11 months, it would have reached a point of increased health and ultimately positive health by the end of year 4. This is very similar to the close call scenario except that the former actually had enough cash to pull through.

In this forecast scenario, it's important to assess how much additional cash would be needed to survive and the likelihood that the current input metrics can hold consistent or improve to ensure the long term success as indicated. This is where the information in the Forecast Summary Box becomes useful, as it will identify the additional reserves required to survive.

This is a challenging scenario to be facing since it is clear that you cannot survive operating as is; however, there's a dangling carrot that says you might be able to make it work. One of the key elements to assess here is an evaluation of how much investment is already at risk and how much more investment would be required to take a shot at success. I would recommend focusing very hard to positively impact the input metrics so that there becomes less ambiguity for future success; plus it may be possible that this could reduce the additional capital required to reach the equilibrium state.

The Unhealthy Success

In the world of successful businesses, there exists the set of companies that are a misleading success, or what I would call an unhealthy success. We often associate a successful business as one that survives the test of time. While this may be a socially accepted definition of success, our discussion of a healthy business here is about financial success. Therefore, a business must deliver back a return on the investment to be successful. See chart [10.6] below as an example of a business that survives the time test, but not the financial test:

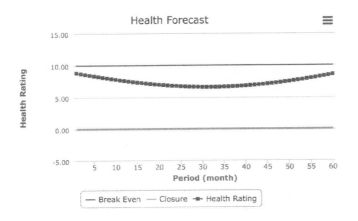

As you can see in the chart, the business is able to cover expenses even in year five, but has yet to be able to return the investment made in the business. This is not an uncommon scenario today; in fact, too many public businesses experience this situation in my opinion. You may have even seen several cases of this, especially in technology, where investors pour money into a business even though the business either operates at a loss or only small profits, all with the vision that one day the company will be worth much, much more. This scenario is extremely prevalent in small businesses, as entrepreneurs keep a business alive by continuing to leverage personal assets; unwilling to let go, but unclear on how to change the trajectory – hence the purpose of this book.

Now, in the example above, we can see that the business has reached equilibrium, since the slope of the health rating reaches consistency before the end of the forecast. This means that the business will eventually operate at a profit; and at some point in time, this business will pass the critical health rating of 10 mark, assuming the metrics don't change. For example, what happens when demand changes or a new competitor comes in? Can the business continue on this path long enough to reach the healthy point?

The question to consider in this scenario becomes where to best place investment dollars. If the goal is to see a return on investment in 5 years or less, then this is not the best of options. However, if you have patience, this could be an acceptable investment. The alternative view is that there is still opportunity to make this business healthy faster by positively impacting the input metrics. Therefore, leverage simulations to identify the most optimal way to achieve a positive health rating sooner.

The Silent Killer

This is one of the most interesting scenarios and a great illustration of why business health monitoring is so critical for any business, even those that appear to be healthy and growing. In this scenario the business is subject to a major inflection point in the health forecast curve based on the relationships of the input metrics. As a result, the once successful business unexpectedly takes a massive downturn; well, unexpected if they were not performing health monitoring.

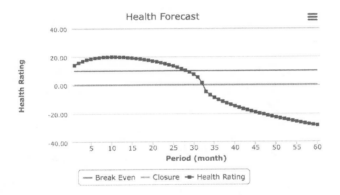

As you can see in the above chart [10.7], the business starts in period 1 with a positive and rapidly growing health rating. Then, just 12 months later, the business begins to decline almost as rapidly. The business continues to decline and is then forced to shut down only 20 months after its peak. This is the silent killer since the business has a condition in the input metrics that will lead to serious negative impact. All too often business leaders don't bother to evaluate a business in this state because it appears quite favorable in the moment. This could just as easily be called the "rock band" scenario. How often do music artists become extremely popular and within a year or two they are no longer a success? Many things can drive this situation for any business, but one of the key drivers is the relationship between customer acquisition and customer attrition.

It could be argued that every successful, thriving business has a forecast that takes a similar shape, except that it may be years before the slope of the health forecast shifts downward; or that the rate of decline may take years rather than months. Great companies, however, find ways to reinvent themselves and thus shift the shape of the curve each time. On the flip side, some companies turn to our government to bail them out...I know, cheap shot. But the point is that even the largest of companies can find themselves in this situation.

One of the key influences to this type of forecast curve is related to consumer demand shifts. Understanding this demand shift as early as possible can be very powerful and provide a significant competitive advantage. Many companies fail to recognize this coming decline in advance, and thus do not have enough time to react. Blockbuster is a great example of such a scenario. Blockbuster failed to recognize that the demand for video rentals from brick and mortar would become nearly obsolete. As a result, services offering direct mail video rental like Netflix and low cost, highly convenient rental kiosks like Redbox became the new age standard, quickly consuming Blockbuster's market share. Add to this the ability to stream movies online due to the advent of high speed internet and Blockbuster, as they originally operated for decades, became extinct. Today, their brand name has been bought and is now fighting to stay alive in the streaming world. This is exactly why health monitoring is important for any business, existing or startup. Neither today's annual profits, nor how long you've been in business, guarantees you success and existence tomorrow. Therefore, you must understand your health at all times and watch out for "the silent killer".

The Ski Hill

The last scenario I want to discuss is mostly relevant to existing businesses rather than startups, as it implies that you are starting from a healthy state. Although, it could apply to any business that is using current financials as the benchmark metrics. In any case, with this scenario the business is on a path of continual decline as in the following chart [10.8]:

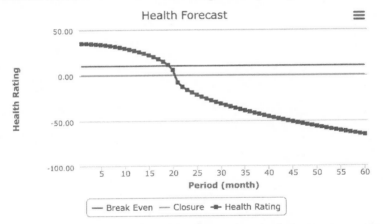

As you can see in this example, the business starts at a healthy level, but it is continually on a downward trend. I call it the Ski Hill because it's kind of like skiing in that when you get off the ski lift and stand at the top of the hill, everything looks so amazing - beautiful views and an exciting run in front of you. Then you start down the hill and are so caught up enjoying the journey that you forget that your elevation is changing. Before you know it, the run is over and your journey has come to an end. While that is the objective of skiing, to continually decline, I hope that's not what you're shooting for in your business. If so, you should stop reading this book and spend your time actually skiing, as I think that will be a great way to achieve your business objective; and much more fulfilling in the end.

In many cases, a business leader may know that the current trajectory is downward. However, this is not always true, as many times as long as bills are getting paid, the leader's focus is elsewhere. Or, if challenges are known, there's a level of overly optimistic thinking that business will turn around soon. If this is your forecast, don't leave the trajectory up to chance. Take control of the metrics that can alter the current path, as we'll discuss in the next chapter.

Your forecast should look visually similar to one of the scenarios presented in this chapter. The exact slopes of your health forecast will differ, as well as the exact health rating values, but ultimately you should be able to relate to one of the above. Regardless of which of the previous forecast scenarios represents the state of your business, the health curve can easily shift to another scenario, positively or negatively, based on changes in the input metrics. Therefore, it will be important that you have fully assessed the risk factors of your business, and specifically factors that will negatively impact your input metrics. As part of this assessment, you can test and evaluate impact of such changes through simulations, which leads us to chapter eleven.

CHAPTER ELEVEN

SIMULATION

Now that you've pulled all the pieces together to compute and evaluate your health forecast, it's time to review your input metrics and the elements that influence these metrics to identify potential risk areas to your business. DO NOT SKIP THIS CHAPTER! While there are elements of tactical execution that as a leader you may find irrelevant for your role, the fundamental strategic process that is presented is critical for your organization to implement. It is this process that will help your organization identify the hidden conditions that pose risk to your business.

An item should be considered risky if it has a lot of variability, is subject to significant negative change in the near future, or if it could cause drastic impact if even just slightly altered. Any time a metric is considered to be risky, you should use the health monitoring software to simulate the impact of possible metric changes; simulating both positive and negative changes. This will be important in helping you to identify and focus on what can be done to improve the health of your business; either to improve from its current state or to offset known or possible negative changes in other input metrics. In the rest of this chapter we will discuss how to assess risk factors for your business and then how

141

to use the simulation capabilities of the Misaic Business Health Monitor to evaluate changes in input metrics.

Assessing Risk Factors

An item that has a large amount of variability from customer to customer or period to period poses a risk since the data, while on average may be acceptable for sustainability, suggests that at any point a series of unfavorable values could appear, resulting in a significant impact on the business. For example, if the effectiveness of a marketing activity has a lot of variability, this makes planning a marketing strategy based on this activity difficult as it has little predictability on future success.

The best way to overcome highly variable metrics is to do deeper dives to understand possible factors that drive the variance and then find ways to assess and control the value of these factors. Advanced processes and data models to identify these factors fall into the concept of predictive modeling, a topic beyond the scope of this book.

Without advanced modeling, there are ways to identify areas of risk so you can at least use your own judgment to determine which factors are most critical. One of the ways to make this assessment is to look at the amount of variability of each input metric and evaluate how common it is for the metric to be less favorable than the expected metric used in the health forecast. If there is a large amount of variability, then this would represent a risk to your assessment of the health forecast.

Make sure your variability is evaluated within the context of any seasonality or segments created as part of your health rating computations. For example, suppose you have a seasonal business such that 3 months out of the year your business declines 50%. If your business in total has variability in sales as a result of peak vs. off-peak seasons, then the variability may not be a concern; so long as the peak and non-peak segment views each have small variability. However, if your peak season has 50% variability, then this would be a concerning risk.

Review each of your highly variable metrics and consider their unfavorable measures as potential risk items to consider in the simulation activities that will follow. Even if some of the variability has not occurred recently, it should be identified as a possible event that could happen on a more recent and frequent basis, influencing the expected value of that metric.

The second consideration in risk factor assessment is any known potential changes to one or more of the input metrics, including acquisition rate, acquisition cost, customer revenue, attrition or operating costs. Going back to our real estate example, had Bob known in advance that ABC Mortgage Experts was going out of business, he could have tried to predict what would happen to his business when that occurs. The analysis should have been quite clear in his case, and he could have started building new marketing strategies in advance to support the business post ABC's closure.

Following are some examples of conditions or factors that can negatively impact your input metrics:

Acquisition Rate
- A new competitor has opened up in the local market

- Approaching full capacity for new customers (eg. church, sports club, etc.)
- Local market opportunity has been reached
- A marketing campaign is about to expire

Acquisition Cost
- Online advertising costs rise as search term bidding increases
- Print or local advertising rates increase
- Increase in marketing required as current marketing is not productive enough
- Expansion to new markets (as local market opportunity is exhausted), requiring a sales manager to support the sales team

Customer Revenue
- Competition is forcing prices downward
- Costs of goods are rising due to supplier price increases
- Economic conditions are reducing customer budgets
- Customers are shopping more at competitors, reducing total spend with your business

Attrition
- Product has limited life cycle (education, sports clubs, etc.)
- New competition in the marketplace
- Recent product defects impacting customer satisfaction

Operations Costs
- Rent increases
- Cost of factory equipment

- Need for incremental office, retail or warehouse space to support growth
- Staff turnover

While the examples above all represent negative influences, most of these have an inverse, or set of positive influences, that can be simulated as well which we'll cover shortly. To prepare for the simulation exercises, we'll create a metric risk assessment grid. This grid will help consolidate the areas of risk and identify the most likely and most impactful changes.

To create the metric risk assessment grid, for each area of key input metrics, including reserves and inventory, layout all the possible negative influences that either you already know are coming or may be possible. Record the current value of that metric as it would be computed for the health rating forecast; remember this is typically the smoothed value.

Next, decide if you know the exact amount of the change, or if you have a better estimate of the percentage change expected. Depending on which value you best understand, compute the math to determine the other. For example, if you know a metric will incur a 10% increase, then multiply the current value by 10% to get the expected value. Alternatively, if you know a metric with a value of $40 will increase to $48, then perform the math to determine the percent increase of 20%. Finally, rate the likelihood that potential change will happen. This can be as simple as using a high, medium or low classification. When complete you should have a grid that resembles the following:

Metric Category	Current Value	Expected Change %	Expected Value	Likelihood of Occurrence
Operating Cost - Rent Increase	$2500/month	20%	$3000/month	High
Acquisition Rate - New Competitor	5% of total customers	-1%	4% of total customers	Medium
Acquisition Rate - Several periods had poor acquisition	5% of total customers	-4%	1% of total customers	Medium
Customer Revenue ($ per customer) - New Competitor	$35/month	-29%	$25/month	Medium
Attrition - New Competitor	3% of total customers	1%	4% of total customers	Medium
Customer Revenue (COGS) - Increase in COGS	$35/month	-9%	$32/month	Low

Now, your table will likely contain a lot more risks and you will want to include more details on each risk; allowing you to better track against these risk factors and to communicate these risks internally. For example, we can see in the grid that COGS might go up. You should include more details than what is listed above, such as which components, what supplier and why do we think costs will go up. This line item instead might say 'We expect

ACME supplier to raise the cost of our t-shirts because every 2-3 years they typically institute a price increase around $3.'

Creating the metric risk assessment grid is a critical exercise to promote business success as it provides the foundation for running simulations and continuously monitoring the health of your business. As part of this process, it forces you to spend time thinking about the risk factors to your business, which quite honestly, many leaders do not spend enough time on since they're so busy trying to run the day to day. This is one of the most important activities that will set you apart from your competition. If you are able to proactively identify risks and put mitigations in place ahead of time, you'll be in a better position than your competition if/when these events transpire.

Identifying Opportunities

Just as we created a metric risk assessment grid, we'll create a metric opportunity grid. This grid will follow the same principles as the risk assessment, except that we'll focus on positive influences to our input metrics. The first part of the opportunities will focus on where certain metrics have significant positive differences from the expected value. For example, if the customer acquisition average is 10 customers per month, but we saw a particular period where we achieved 20 customers, we'll want to highlight this. The objective then is to evaluate the cause for that variance and determine if it can be repeated consistently or not. Maybe that period you tried a new online marketing campaign and it was particularly successful. If it is reasonable that repeating this activity can produce similar results, then this could be an opportunity to consider in simulation.

After reviewing above average historical occurrences, move on to identify known or potential changes to the business that would positively impact the health rating. Below are some examples that could be favorable influences to input metrics:

Acquisition Rate

- Increase in marketing budget or new marketing activities planned
- Entry into a new market or distribution channel
- New partnership that is expected to generate incremental business
- Closing of a local competitor

Acquisition Cost

- Identification of lower cost marketing channels such as social media (Facebook, LinkedIn, etc.) and/or email marketing
- Increase in customer generation from referrals vs. traditional marketing channels
- Reduction in advertising costs

Customer Revenue

- Planned price increase
- Expansion of products or services (to capture more spend per customer)
- New supplier of raw materials decreasing costs of goods sold

<u>Attrition</u>
- Increase in customer satisfaction as identified by a recent survey
- New contract policies requiring long term customer commitment
- Product offering changes, creating a truly distinct and valuable competitive advantage

<u>Operating Costs</u>
- Rent decreases through negotiation or relocation
- Reduction in cost of factory equipment
- Reduction in operating staff through planned automation

Again, your list will likely be much more extensive, but recognize that there are many factors that can positively influence your health rating. Once you've identified your list, create an opportunity grid just like the risk assessment grid, except this grid will contain the favorable influencers. While you certainly can combine both risks and opportunities onto one grid, I recommend having two separate grids just for clarity between the favorable and unfavorable influencers to your input metrics.

Initial Simulations

Now that you've created your metric risk assessment and opportunity grids, you are ready to begin simulating these scenarios. The process of simulation should be relatively easy to implement using the simulation capabilities of the Misaic Business Health Monitor. Simply replace the current average value used in the forecast with the future expected value as recorded in the risk assessment grid or opportunity grid. This will generate a new health forecast which you can compare to the original forecast to identify the impact. We'll review how to do this within the software later in this chapter.

As you begin the simulation process, start by changing only one metric at a time and then record the impact to the health rating as a new column on your respective risk or opportunity grid. Begin with all the isolated risk simulations first, and then do the isolated opportunity simulations. In this case, you would add a column called "isolated impact" and record the impact as high, medium or low. This will enable you to see which items pose the biggest risk or opportunity to the business on their own, so you can plan action steps accordingly as we'll discuss in chapter twelve. This is an important part of the simulation exercise since even though a risk or opportunity may be highly likely to occur, it may not be very impactful to the overall business. Whereas, something that may be somewhat unlikely could have a major impact, altering the business's future outlook. This on its own is a very powerful picture to have.

You may want to add an additional column that describes what the impact is more tangibly. For example, you might say "health rating reaches 0 in 10 months" or "shift from ideal state curve to close call, bottoming out in month 8". This would allow you to better understand the severity of two different high impact items.

The next simulation will identify the effect of the most impactful risks occurring together. Add another column to the grid calling it "most impactful risks-simultaneous impact", and input a level of impact of high, medium or low as appropriate. Add a details column to capture more information on the impact of this simulation exercise. If the most impactful risks combined together do not produce an unfavorable health forecast, then you are likely in a really good position. It doesn't mean you don't need to be concerned with the risks, but the outlook for the business is good.

Next, move onto the most impactful opportunities. Follow the same steps as with most impactful risks except only change the input metrics for the most impactful opportunities; add both a "most impactful opportunities-simultaneous impact" and a details column. If the result of this simulation results in anything except the ideal state or typical startup forecast, this warrants some serious concern for the business - as it means even if everything went right the business is still unhealthy.

The next simulation exercise is to change the values for items in the risk grid that are highly likely to occur; add both a "most likely risks-simultaneous impact" and a details column. Following the same process, replace current values with expected values only for the risks that are likely to occur and update your forecast accordingly. The resulting forecast now represents a likely state of the business if nothing else were to change favorably as identified in the opportunities grid.

Continuing forward, simulate the impact of only the most likely opportunities expected to occur; add both a "most likely opportunities-simultaneous impact" and a details column. The resulting forecast represents a likely state of the business if nothing else were to change negatively as stated in the risks grid.

To complete the high level evaluation, we will simulate the impact of the most likely risks and opportunities together. Once again, adding appropriate new columns to the grid for "most likely forecast-simultaneous impact" as well as a respective details column. (Since this simulation incorporates metrics from both grids, I might include it on the risk grid, but the choice is up to you.) The resulting forecast represents a likely state of the business based on both risks and opportunities that are most likely to occur.

After completing these initial simulations, you will have a good starting point to understand the potential future health of your business. Furthermore, you'll be able to now identify which of the risks and opportunities will be the most relevant to focus on as you take action, which we'll discuss in chapter twelve.

Now, you're probably saying to yourself that reality will likely result in a mixture of some of the risks and some of the opportunities coming to fruition. That is correct. However, for this first round of simulation it's important to identify the isolated impacts of each of these, so as events occur, you already know the likely impact to the business.

The following table summarizes the initial simulation steps:

Initial Simulations	
Step 1:	Iterate through each risk measuring the impact of each risk in isolation
Step 2:	Iterate through each opportunity measuring the impact of each opportunity in isolation
Step 3:	Evaluate the most impactful risks resulting from step 1 simultaneously
Step 4:	Evaluate the most impactful opportunities resulting from step 2 simultaneously
Step 5:	Evaluate the most likely risks simultaneously
Step 6:	Evaluate the most likely opportunities simultaneously
Step 7:	Evaluate the most likely scenario combining most likely risks and opportunities simultaneously

Iterative Simulations

After completing the initial simulation scenarios, you should have a good understanding of what is going to heavily influence your health forecast. The next part of the simulation process will be to run numerous iterations of differing scenarios so that you can develop relevant targets for action planning. For example, in the initial simulations we used estimated future values based on the risk assessment or opportunity grid. However, what if the actual future values fall between the current value and the expected value? It's important to understand at what threshold of change does the impact significantly alter your forecast or business outlook.

In addition to simulating varying levels of expected values for each metric, there's also the numerous permutations of different risks and opportunities occurring together. There is no correct number of simulations to run; but at a minimum, I would certainly spend the effort to cover off as many iterations of the high impact and high likelihood items as possible.

One of the main objectives of running iterative simulations is to identify ways to offset unfavorable metric influencers with other metric changes. For example, let's say you've identified your rent is going to increase $1,000. This is going to negatively impact the health forecast. However, through simulation you identify that if you could increase your customer acquisition rate by 2 customers per month, you can keep your health forecast stable. Alternatively, by increasing revenue per customer by $2, you can also achieve a neutral impact from the rent increase. Or, maybe it's a combination of both the number of new customers and revenue per customer that will keep the business headed in the right direction.

As you run through your simulation iterations, it will be important to keep track of the most relevant combinations of metric changes to preserve or improve your health. Relevant combinations need to be comprised of metric changes that are based on realistic external influences, that is changes that are possible to occur, or as a result of internal execution of achievable action plans. For example, it is not realistic to say "if we just double the number of new customers per month", if there is no tangible action plan that can be executed to produce such results. Certainly, if you run a TV advertisement you might be able to create significant traffic, however, is there really a budget for such an advertisement? And don't forget, you need to include the costs of executing action plans into your input metrics.

The Online Simulation Tool

Running through a variety of simulation scenarios can be time consuming; however, it is an exercise well worth the investment. Just remember the more you know and understand about your key metrics, the more effective you can be at planning, thus increasing the chances of improving your business health. In order to simplify this process and ensure that every business has the ability to simulate metric changes, the free edition of the Misaic Business Health Monitor includes a simulation tool.

To utilize the simulation capabilities within the Misaic Business Health Monitor, simply login to your account to get to the home forecast screen. In the Forecast Summary Box you will see a toggle switch to turn the simulator on/off. When you switch it to on, you will see the 'Update' button turn green. Simply click the update button and the forecasting capabilities will now appear. The resulting screen should look similar to illustration [11.1] that follows:

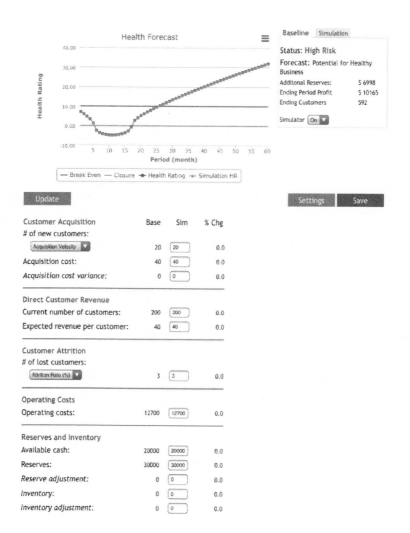

As you activate the simulator, it will automatically copy the baseline forecast metrics into the column for the simulation metrics, labeled 'Sim', and as a result, the values in the '% Chg' column will all equal 0. You will also notice that the Forecast Summary Box now has an additional tab for Simulation which we'll get to shortly. Additionally, the chart has now added another line for the 'Simulation HR', which by default has the same metrics as the Baseline Health Rating, so the two lines will overlap until differences exist in the metrics. Notice in the Forecast Summary Box above, the current baseline forecast requires an additional $6,998 of reserves to survive the period where the forecast drops below 0.

You will now be able to change the input metrics to the health formula in the 'Sim' column while the baseline metrics remain fixed so you know where you started. As you make changes to the Simulation values, you will see the '% Chg' column automatically update so you are aware how big of a change you are suggesting. Again, you will not be able to notice the color coding in print here, but '% Chg' values are displayed as green for increases and red for decreases. Change the relevant metrics and click update to see the impact. See the following illustration [11.2]:

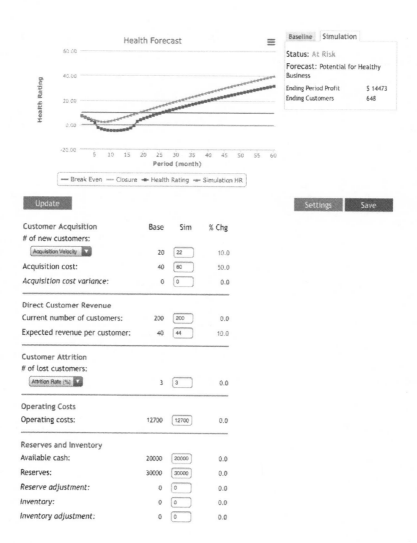

In the example above, you will see that the business is suggesting increasing acquisition costs by 50% (investing in more marketing) in hopes to increase new customers by 10%. Additionally, the business is anticipating increasing customer revenue by $4 or 10% (possibly through a price increase). If these metric values can be achieved, the outlook for the business changes dramatically.

First, we can see the business no longer drops below the 0 health rating, meaning the risk of closure has been reduced and there is no longer a need for additional reserves; however, given how closely the simulation forecast approaches zero, and the high risk of the baseline forecast, I would still be prepared to infuse more capital. Next, we can identify from the chart that the baseline forecast indicates the company will not be in a healthy state until just after 2 years. However, with the simulated scenario, the business reaches a healthy state within 18 months.

Finally, we can notice in the baseline forecast tab in illustration [11.1] that ending profit per period is about $10,000 per month. By looking at the Ending Period Profit in the simulation tab from illustration [11.2], we can see that profits now reach more than $14,000 per period, a 40% increase. In this simple example, we can see the power of simulation to identify how specific actions can transform the trajectory of the business.

Used appropriately, simulation can be the most powerful roadmap for strategic planning purposes and determining the business's path to success; but it must be accompanied by good business judgment. Follow the simulation process outlined in this chapter to identify the key risks and opportunities that exist, including both the obvious and the hidden. Keep in mind that input metrics need to be achievable and the expected or anticipated results should be carefully evaluated. It's always best to use history or research data to support proper input metric values whenever possible. Remember that forecasting is based on the input metrics, which may vary in their accuracy or stability.

Finally, simulation based on the past does not account for unexpected future events that can alter results drastically from what was expected. Because of this, it's important to review your forecasts monthly rather than periodically. This is the best way to ensure that any anomalies or drastic changes in the business are recognized early, allowing you to react accordingly in a timely matter.

CHAPTER TWELVE

TAKING ACTION

If you complete the processes described up through chapter eleven, chances are, you will have more knowledge about your business than ever before. In fact, you will most likely understand your business better than any of your competitors understand theirs. You should understand your customer's purchase behavior, the overall health forecast for your business, the key influencers to your company's future success, and critical metric focus points to steer your business towards an even healthier state. All this knowledge is incredibly powerful and a true competitive advantage. However, unless you take action against this information, it will not change the fate of your business. So, let's discuss the last step of the process, executing on these powerful insights.

As simple as it may sound, executing can actually be quite challenging as it takes effort, planning, commitment, resources and focus. When a business is operating at full capacity, it can seem impossible to find the time, money and/or people to help institute changes; especially if the results are not immediate. Don't let your business fall into the trap of saying "we'll get to that soon", as you'll find there's never a good time. Then, before you know it, it's too late. Instead, remind yourself that you set down the journey of reading this book because you had a true interest in the long term survival of your business. Today's heroics of running the business will be forgotten in short time and are irrelevant if the business is not around in a few years or less.

Let's shift our focus to turning our simulation exercises into tangible action plans to drive successful outcomes. Now, at first glance it might be quite obvious what needs to be done as the simulations actually describe the goal. For example, to offset the coming rent increase we need to improve our customer acquisition rate by X%. However, while this is the clear answer of <u>what</u> to achieve, the question remains "<u>how</u> do I change the metric values?" I want to spend the rest of the chapter providing some ideas on how you might go about impacting each of the input metrics. Therefore, we will need to focus a bit deeper than just the metric itself in order to influence it.

Customer Acquisition

For any business, generating new customers is going to be important to sustaining and improving overall business health. Some businesses lend themselves better than others to acquiring new customers as a result of the target audience or market demand. Some businesses naturally lend themselves to word of mouth exposure, and some can be explained and differentiated easily through print advertisements. Regardless of business differences, here are some consistent ways you can impact and improve your acquisition rate and costs:

<u>Referral Program</u>: Referral programs can increase customer acquisition rates and reduce your acquisition costs dramatically. Your customers can be your best sales associates. Customers, as a whole, have a huge network and can provide exposure to more potential customers than traditional advertising. Also, since customers have used the product or service, they can often explain it better than any print mediums. Finally, referrals are typically free; but don't hold back from rewarding customers, as that can increase their incentive to mention your company to their network. If you have an incentive attached, it becomes a pay for performance marketing system that pays for itself without risk. Also, a well-designed referral system scales with your business.

<u>Marketing Effectiveness Measurement</u>: Another way to improve your acquisition metrics is through marketing effectiveness measurement. One of the most commonly missed opportunities in businesses is maximizing marketing spend. I suggest that the two biggest contributors to this is either lack of focus or lack of knowledge/processes to measure effectiveness. Much of the lack of focus happens because business leaders are too busy managing the day to day operations so there is no time to sit down and understand which marketing mediums are truly the most effective. Sometimes lack of focus occurs because leaders feel they have a sense for which activities work best based on their experience hearing how customers are generated. However, this is not the same as identifying actual ROI (return on investment) on marketing activities or analyzing which marketing activities generate

different customer profiles. The other challenge for business leaders is knowing how to assess effectiveness. This occurs either because the data is not there to support analysis or the owner is not skilled in analyzing the data. As you implement marketing effectiveness analysis in your business here are a few tips to keep in mind:

- Use promotion codes on all your advertising activities so you can identify which source customers are coming from
- Analyze information by product and customer segments so you can better select marketing activities that are appropriate to support your targeted action plans
- Make sure you incorporate the long term value of your customer in assessing if a marketing activity is effective. Note, some activities might bring a lot of new customers, but if those attracted by the offer never repeat purchase, the mechanism may not be effective for long term success. It might even be worth looking at cohorts by marketing activity.
- Include referrals as a marketing activity, tracking and measuring its effectiveness just like traditional marketing. At the same time, make sure that any referral rewards align to the value of new customers; it may even be worth testing the long term value of referral customers vs. non-referral customers.

Sales Team Effectiveness: Having a sales team is not the same as having an effective sales team. Similar to measuring the effectiveness of your marketing activities, you should be measuring the effectiveness of your sales team and looking for opportunities to improve overall sales performance. In some cases, it could be a matter of increasing speed of response to online inquiries. Studies have shown that the company to respond first is more likely to win the sale, regardless of price or product differences. Another big area of opportunity is in follow-up activities. Many companies collect endless inquiries, but fail to continue beyond the first attempt at a sale. Ensure you have a proper CRM system in place to not only collect sales leads, but also track and measure against the sales activities. Finally, identify if there are gaps in training that could be driving performance differences. Training can vary from product training to sales training. In any case, make sure to maximize the investment you're making in a sales team.

Social Media: It's likely no surprise that social media is on the list. Social media sites, including powerhouses like Facebook and LinkedIn, are growing by the masses. These are very low cost mediums that have broad coverage, yet can reach targeted audiences. But don't limit yourself to just these two popular sites. Look for trade specific sites that you can connect into, often providing an opportunity to contribute via online forums, articles, and blogs relevant to your customers. If you have a business to business product, then local chamber of commerce sites may provide a place for you to connect to your target audience through such online forums.

Online Marketing: Another avenue of customer acquisition that is often underutilized by small businesses is online marketing. There are many aspects to online marketing, and technically social media could be classified here; but the difference surrounds passive marketing vs. interactive as I'm suggesting in the social media space. Within online marketing, some areas of focus to evaluate are your search engine optimization (SEO) and lead generation avenues (such as google ad words), as these can drastically boost traffic directly to your website. But before increasing traffic to your website, you need to ensure that your website is truly designed to serve as a sales tool. Equip your site with captivating videos and blogs/articles to provide value to your potential customers. Even further, offer something of value in exchange for a visitor's email address so that you can market directly to them. This is a very low cost way to potentially convert traffic from your website into new customers. Leverage these same videos by posting them on You Tube as another free advertising channel. This type of optimization will not only help generate traffic from web searchers, but will help increase conversion from customer referrals who start exploring your company by visiting your website. Finally, make sure you are properly tracking and analyzing your web traffic, continually looking for ways to improve conversion.

While there are many ways to improve your customer acquisition rate and costs, it's important to identify relevant opportunities for your business, define goals and targets, and execute and track against your objectives. While customer acquisition is always important, it is especially critical for businesses that have short customer lifespans by nature as natural attrition will occur, leaving the only hope for long term success driven by a constant flow of new customers.

Customer Revenue

It could be argued that increasing customer revenue is the most important focus for long term success. The reason that this is so important is that the amount a customer spends with you is their economic vote of how much they like your products and services. The more a customer spends, the more valuable you are to them (in your business category) and it indicates the customer's level of loyalty to you. As you build customer loyalty over time, price becomes less of a decision factor for the customer as there is an inherent value to an expectation of quality and satisfaction. Customers will often pay more for products and services if they have trust in the provider. This gives you an additional lever for business growth as you have more flexibility for future price increases since your demand curve is a bit more inelastic. Remember, that by customer revenue here we are referring to direct customer revenue, so we're not only focused on how much a customer spends, but also how much direct revenue you obtain from the transaction. Here are some focus areas to improve customer revenue:

Product Expansion: Creating a broader selection of products or services enables your existing customers to spend more with you. This works especially well if you can complement existing products with other products that your customer would have purchased anyway. Major retailers such as Walmart and

167

Target have embraced this concept by expanding their offering to include groceries at many of their retail stores. The result is more dollars per transaction from existing customers, while at the same time, customers get a benefit of convenience by getting their shopping complete at one store. Another expansion approach is to offer alternative products that can generate more revenue than current products. For example, expanding a hot dog menu to include Italian beef may shift purchasing from a $1.99 hot dog to a $4.99 beef. This example is a perfect demonstration of why we focus on direct customer revenue. If the hot dog yields a $1.59 profit while the beef only yields a profit of $1.10, this could actually negatively impact the health of your business if the customer merely swaps products. However, adding beef to the menu could add meal variety for the customer and actually increase the number of trips she makes to your store in a monthly period, increasing your overall revenue per customer. Look for relevant product expansion opportunities, being very conscious of how the addition of such products may cannibalize other offerings and how direct customer revenue may be impacted.

Promotions: Expanding product offerings may increase transactions per customer as in the beef example above; however, look for other ways to increase transactions per customer. The more times you can get customers to transact with you, the more revenue you will earn and the more loyalty you'll build. Promotions are a great way to get customers to purchase above their normal purchase cycle amounts. These can come in many forms including: discounts on products with a minimum purchase, discounts to try new products (building on the product expansion opportunity discussed above), or could consist of a significant discount which is offered to the customer after they have reached their typical spend. While promotions can be very effective at generating incremental revenue, be careful as they are often misused and instead reduce revenue per customer. For example, providing $2.00 off an order when the customer would have purchased the same items anyway is actually harmful to the health rating. The more you know about your customers' purchase behavior, the smarter you can be about the offers you provide to them. Using advanced data modeling you can actually determine whether or not a customer promotion is incremental or cannibalistic to revenue. Look to design promotions using an understanding of your customers' behavior and be sure to track whether or not your promotions are positively changing direct customer revenue.

Packages (Pre-paid): Some businesses have regular purchase cycles that vary significantly by customer, such as haircuts, oil changes and even pizza. In these cases, it may be worthwhile to offer pre-paid packages that force the behavior that you want your customer to exhibit. Using an oil change business as an example, imagine offering 10% off oil changes if a customer purchases 4 oil changes at one time, which must be used within 12 months. This forces the customer to come back every three months versus every four or five. Now, take a customer that tends to come back 30 days late for each of their oil changes. In a 2 year period, this means they would complete 6 oil changes versus the recommended 8. However, by offering 10% off and forcing 4 oil changes per year, total customer spend increases from 6 oil changes to 8 oil changes, a 33% increase in 24 months for a cost of 10%. This is a net increase of 23% by merely encouraging more regular visits. And, because the customer has pre-purchased their oil changes, they are unlikely to switch to a competitor, helping to reduce attrition further. In the end, the customer gets a discount, their car is in a better condition, customer revenue increases by 23%, and attrition decreases. This type of creative thinking is how you can create win-win marketing strategies. While pre-paid packages do not work for every business, there may be other types of packages that you can create to increase the number of customer transactions or total spend per customer.

Pricing: An obvious way to increase revenue per customer is to increase your prices. This is always a difficult decision for businesses since most do not actually have a good understanding of their product price elasticity. Highly elastic products will have a significant drop in demand as a result of price increases as compared to inelastic products. In the absence of not knowing your price elasticity, how do you make a decision to change prices? Here are a few tips that can help you make pricing changes and minimize potential negative consequences:

- If possible, try implementing control and test scenarios to see if price changes impact purchase behavior.
- Utilize product affinities to identify associated products and, at a given point in time, only alter pricing for one of

several products highly associated together. This way, you will likely not lose all the revenue if customers respond negatively. Additionally, the price impact will not be as drastic to customers as only part of a typical purchase transaction will have increased.

- Provide coupons for a period of time on the products that have increased in price, so that while the price has clearly increased, the net price is the same to the customer. This will help the customer adapt to the new price schema.
- If a product has a large set of customers that only purchase that item, make sure that your adjusted price remains competitive in the marketplace so those customers do not defect. Also, if your targeted price increase items are below market, this may potentially be the reason a key set of customers are shopping with you. Be careful. It may make sense to grow those customers into more product lines first, and instead, focus on other areas to increase price.

Cost Analysis: Reducing any direct costs will improve direct customer revenue and in turn, the health of your business. In order to change costs, you will need to look at the current suppliers, business processes and labor costs to identify where opportunities for improvement might exist. Determining where to begin can be daunting, so I suggest starting first with any product segment that has a negative health rating. If you cannot improve this product segment, then it may be worth eliminating this product or service from your portfolio, unless it is a strategic loss leader. If it is a loss leader, I would be sure to utilize affinity analysis to ensure that this item is associated with overall profitable items and transactions. The next area I would move to is your highest volume product segments since small changes to these segments can add up to huge improvements. Following the high volume products I would look at areas where things are not currently working well; whether that be bad suppliers, poor resource performers, or processes that seem to fail or cause problems. Fixing these may not only yield lower costs, but can reduce "time suck" activities, freeing up resources for other use. Finally, move on to other areas of the business that were not mentioned in the groups listed here. While this is a suggested work flow to identify areas for cost improvements, use your judgment to determine the best approach to find ways to reduce direct costs.

Customer Attrition

One of the easiest ways to improve the health of your business is to reduce your attrition rate. The reason I consider this an easy opportunity is that it is significantly harder to acquire customers than it is to retain them. Also, retaining a customer has long term value from both continued income and growth that results from referrals. Therefore, even small improvements in attrition can yield exponential results. Another reason that a focus on attrition is so important is that attrition is often one of the biggest factors in "the silent killer" scenario. A sudden or significant shift in demand for your products or services can be detrimental. As we previously discussed, there are two different types of attrition that we need to consider, natural and elective attrition. The following are some ways to help manage attrition:

<u>Surveys</u>: It will be critical to implement surveys in order to best understand the reasons that customers have defected. Again, these surveys can be via phone, text, email, or direct mail, with phone surveys being the best option if possible. This will help you make sure you are focusing on the right issues to help manage attrition. Also, be sure to do regular satisfaction surveys for existing customers as this will give good insights as to why customers might be defecting, or even help prevent attrition by catching concerns and opportunities in advance.

<u>Price Matching</u>: Consumers are notorious for looking to get the best deal possible; there's nothing new about that. However, the accessibility of information with modern technology changes the pricing game for many businesses. Consumers have access to a plethora of data to find the best prices out there for "commodity like" items. In fact, consumers are often looking up competitor prices while shopping in retail stores. As a result, rather than losing the customer to a pricing battle, price matching has almost become a norm. Think about how to incorporate price matching in your business if you are faced with customers defecting due to lower prices. While your product margins may decline on particular items, you will keep your overall customer revenue closer in tact by retaining the rest of the customer's business. Don't be afraid to put restrictions around the price match

policy, such as the items must be in stock at the competitor, the customer must be able to prove the price, etc.

Product Expansion: One of the main causes of natural attrition is that the product or service has a limited life cycle, or at least a significant lapse in time between a typical customer's purchases. If this scenario applies, product expansion could be a successful way to retain customers. For example, consider a lawn care company in the Midwest for which the business is seasonal, typically April through September. An option to maintain connection with customers is to offer a snow removal service, Christmas lighting service, or other type of service that can be performed during the winter months while landscaping is dormant. This helps build loyalty and keeps the company top of mind to prevent competitors from earning the customer's business come spring when landscaping becomes active once again. Product expansion can also be important if customers are defecting because competitors are offering a wider selection of products or complimentary products. All the principles of one stop shopping mentioned earlier in this chapter are also important here in regards to attrition. Having the right product selection maximizes customer revenue, retains customers, and can even be a draw to acquire new customers.

Loyalty Program: Research has proven that loyalty programs are effective at building brand equity, increasing customer spend, and retaining customers. Customers are more likely to shop at merchants for which they belong to a loyalty program.

174

Part of implementing a loyalty program should include constant contact with your customers, which is discussed in more detail next. Beyond the sense of connection that is created as part of a loyalty program, if customers have built up rewards, they may be more likely to come back to your establishment to redeem those rewards. More importantly, a loyalty program will provide detailed customer purchase behavior; allowing you to design more relevant customer offers, increasing the likelihood that a customer transacts business with you. Implementing a loyalty program needs to be well thought out, purposeful, and requires a fair amount of time and commitment; however, most businesses will reap significant rewards long term.

Constant Contact: Don't let your business become forgotten by your customers. Too many businesses take their customer relationships and business for granted. Unless your product is so unique that you have no competition, don't just assume that your customers will remember you or choose to transact business with you. It's critical that you remain top of mind for customers, even if they're not in the market for your offerings at the moment; this is exceptionally critical for products that face natural attrition or long purchase cycles. Remain connected with your customers through the use of promotions, newsletters, emails, blogs, etc. so that you remain relevant to them. This is not only important to keep your customers from defecting to a competitor, but also so that you are more likely to earn a referral when your customer is in conversation with other people in their network that are in the market for your products or services. There are many low cost providers for email marketing and blog services than can help you keep connections strong. You do not need to have a loyalty program in place to maintain constant connection, but a loyalty program is certainly not complete if it does not incorporate constant contact as part of the framework.

Advanced Retention Analysis: A more aggressive and effective approach to proactively getting ahead of attrition is through retention analysis. This more advanced data analysis and modeling approach identifies customer behaviors and factors that are associated with or lead to customer attrition. Using this information, each customer can be assigned a likelihood of defecting, allowing you to get ahead of attrition before it happens through appropriate marketing and communication efforts. You can also track retention techniques to find the most effective methods for retaining customers based on their risk factors.

As discussed earlier, focusing on customer retention, or reducing attrition, is such a valuable opportunity to improve the health of your business, that companies have entire divisions dedicated to this. While you may not require or have the ability to dedicate a large team to this area, it should still be a focus for your business with a clear set of standards, goals, processes and measurement tools in place. Putting an attrition management framework in place will be a key ingredient to the sustainability of your company.

Operating Costs

To this point, we've focused on ways to action against customer based metrics. However, this chapter would not be complete without at least touching on the obvious opportunity to improve business health through focus on operating costs. I find that businesses are most conscious of their operating costs since these are the bills that get paid on a regular basis and thus, are easy metrics to typically get to (compared to customer based metrics). This is not meant to imply that businesses are focusing on improving operating costs, or that the details of the operating cost specifics are known. In any case, let's review a couple of key ways to improve operating costs:

Supplier Review: An obvious way to improve operating costs is to look for ways to reduce expenses by doing a supplier review. Essentially, this means looking at the source for each of the operating costs and determining if there are alternative suppliers for the particular item. This can include rent, supplies, even wages and salaries that are managerial in nature and not directly allocated to the production of goods and services (covered already as part of direct customer revenue). In many cases, operating costs are driven by commodity items that have many suppliers or providers, creating a constantly changing marketplace of prices and offerings. However, many times businesses sign-up for services and do not take the time to revisit the available services 12 or 18 months later, at which point their current provider may be overpriced and/or lacking the more advanced features that can actually increase output or reduce related costs. Spend the time when it's appropriate to look for ways to improve your business health through simple supplier switches. However, be careful that you do not create more challenges or impact quality to your customers in making changes. Reducing costs at the expense of increasing attrition is not a worthwhile tactic.

Process Improvement: Beyond simply changing suppliers, a large portion of businesses have an opportunity to reduce operating costs through process improvement. While we mentioned process improvement for the direct production of goods, this type of process improvement provides impact on a more macro level, such as reducing the need for retail/office/warehouse space or machinery. These are items that are not typically accounted for on a per item basis. For example, Amazon created a complex algorithm that maximizes the storage of goods in its distribution centers. As a result, they have doubled their storage capacity per warehouse, significantly reducing operating costs in each region. Another creative process design is Tesla motors which sells electric cars. Tesla has created a showroom model where customers don't actually purchase the car in the showroom, but rather they buy online. Their unique model ditches the "dealerships in every city" concept and instead focuses on a handful of showrooms for a large geographical area. In fact, they actually have their showrooms inside shopping malls with a car to test drive in the parking lot. Not only does this reduce costs for rent given the significantly less square footage requirements, but because they don't sell vehicles from inside the store, they can remain open on Sundays and gain a unique competitive advantage that most car dealerships do not have...Sunday traffic! Don't underestimate the power of process improvement as it cannot only serve to find ways to reduce costs, but as you can see here it can actually create distinct competitive advantages.

Reserves

Managing reserves is another way to impact the health of your business. The important concept to understand in relation to the health formula is that any time you add reserves to a healthy business, one that has a health rating of 10 or higher, your health rating will decrease. On the contrary, adding reserves to an unhealthy business will improve the health of the business. However, adding reserves will not and cannot mathematically, bring the business from an unhealthy state to a healthy state; in fact, this is the common approach that creates the unhealthy success. With these two principles in mind, and knowing that the inverse of each is true, here are two ways to improve your health rating with caveats to each:

Capital Infusion: If a business is unhealthy, as indicated by a health rating less than 10, increasing reserves through additional cash will increase the health rating. This happens as there is now more working cash to either support, or protect against, unprofitable months. However, just because the health rating improves, it does not mean that the capital infusion is a wise decision. The health forecast will be a critical input to evaluating if the business is worth investing any more cash into. If there is indication that the business can sustain and reach a healthy state (as identified through simulation), then the infusion may be worth the risk. Every situation is extremely unique and there is no clear answer or guarantee. It will be up to the business leaders and investors to evaluate the right decisions given all the information at hand including: simulations, total investment already committed, additional investment required, opportunity costs of the potential new capital, and overall risk adversity of those involved.

Capital Distribution: The direct opposite of infusing capital is to distribute capital back to the owners/investors. Distributing reserves in an unhealthy business will drive the health rating even further down and add risk of failure to the business. If the business is operating at a healthy state, again with a health rating greater than or equal to 10, then distributing this capital will increase the health rating of the company. It's important to make sure the company is not at risk of becoming unhealthy before making such distributions. Additionally, if there is excess cash to invoke a distribution, it is worth simulating the impact of applying those funds into the business to improve any of the health metrics that will also increase the health of the business. For example, could those funds be used to implement a major process improvement that improves direct customer revenue and/or operating costs? Or, could these funds be used to create and implement a loyalty program that improves direct customer revenue and attrition metrics? Again, simulating the impact of such alternatives and assessing the resulting health rating can be a guide to evaluating potential distributions.

As we can see, reserves play an important role in impacting the health rating. While there are no clear cut rules to make the right decision surrounding reserves, it's good to understand that adding reserves to an unhealthy business and distributing reserves from a healthy business will both yield positive health gains. However, it is always important to incorporate the health forecast and simulations to support decisions regarding reserves.

Determining the Action Path

With a handful of approaches available to impact the various input metrics, as described in this chapter or others you develop on your own, the next step will be to determine which actions to take and in what order. Going back to our risk and opportunity grids from chapter eleven, let's append a few more columns. First, for each of the risks and opportunities, let's append "potential mitigation approaches". Here we'll describe the specific mitigation option proposed. Next, let's add the following additional columns to capture for each risk or opportunity: how quickly the mitigations would take to implement, how much cost would be involved, how much effort is required, and how big of an impact to the rest of the business would the actions cause. With these additional parameters added to the grid, you will have a full view of the risks and opportunities along with solutions and impact; giving you the appropriate details to make informed decisions and create data driven action plans.

181

We have reviewed many ways to impact the key metrics that drive the health of your business. There is no silver bullet that will guarantee success, but by identifying the most impactful metrics from simulations, you can have clarity on where to take action first. Then combining some of the recommended actions in this chapter with others that you devise, you can create an action plan to execute. In order to maximize the odds of success, be sure that you create a realistic, actionable project plan, and then track and continuously measure against that plan. To ensure your business has the tools to be successful, I've provided some general guidance for creating a successful project plan in Appendix A. With the knowledge of where to focus your attention and strategies on how to make a meaningful impact on the future of your business, you are now equipped for the final step - take action and create a sustainable, successful business.

CONCLUSION

I set out on a mission with this book to help business owners and leaders become aware of a powerful concept that can drastically impact the future of their companies. Business success or failure does not need to be a result of luck or chance. In fact, the success of a business can be determined formulaically, using a set of clearly defined metrics. Each and every business leader has the capability to use this formula to measure the health of their business and forecast its future. Having this knowledge at hand, along with the understanding of the key factors that drive the forecast, enables you to make proactive decisions that can improve the overall success of your company.

Throughout this book, we utilized metrics that are based on customer analytics; that is, a true understanding of each of your customer's behavior. Generating customer analytics might be a giant step forward on its own, or it may be simply applying these metrics differently than you have before. None of this will come without effort, challenges, and learning...and as a result, both personal and professional growth. I only hope that I was able to communicate with enough clarity and conviction how powerful business health monitoring can be for your business, such that the effort to implement these concepts is clearly worthwhile.

As you take your next steps forward, a few things to keep in mind:

- Maximize the value of your customer data; and if you haven't been collecting customer data, make it a priority.
- Focus on creating customer and product segments to improve the accuracy of your metrics and to create more effective strategies by utilizing knowledge about these segments.
- Make business health monitoring part of your continuous business practice, spending the time to identify the hidden conditions that can lead to business health decline.
- Simulate changes to the critical metrics that can both positively and negatively impact your business health, so you know where to focus to take control of your business's future.
- Don't let the knowledge and insights gained from the business health monitoring process be wasted; create tactical action plans and execute with focus and persistence.
- Finally, share the wisdom with fellow entrepreneurs. We all know someone who is trying to fulfill their dream; you can be the person that helps makes it happen for them.

That's it. You made it through my hybrid business strategy / text book, with a little bit of training thrown in for free. And, while this concludes the book, hopefully it starts a new chapter for your business. If you have questions as you implement business health monitoring within your organization, or if you have any feedback regarding this book, feel free to email me directly at bhm_book@misaic.com. Also, visit www.misaic.com for related articles and blogs that can assist your business.

Best wishes for you and your business ventures, and may you... Survive the Odds!

APPENDIX

APPENDIX A

SUCCESSFUL PROJECT PLANNING

Managing project plans is not necessarily the skill set or desire for many business owners. This is not a bad thing. However, many goals and objectives are missed due to the lack of proper planning. I am not project management certified, nor do I have any desire to be. I cringe at the thought of using formal project management software again, and prefer these days to use spreadsheets to track my plans. However, I have managed and been involved in projects small in nature, as well as massive – to the tune of $100 million plus. Through these experiences, I have learned the common themes that lead to success or failure, regardless of project size. Therefore, this appendix is not meant to be a formal training in project management, but rather some simple tips and recommendations to help ensure you can be successful executing the action steps you identify for your business.

Creating a Formal Plan

In order to be most effective in improving your business health, I recommend putting a formal plan together. By formal plan, I mean a document that can be referenced on a regular basis and shared within your organization as needed. The formal plan will serve as your clearly defined map towards improvement. Just because your plan is documented does not mean it cannot change. In fact, it should be reviewed on a regular basis and modified as appropriate. I recommend that your formal plan contains at least the following three elements:

Project Charter: The project charter serves as the executive summary of what you are trying to accomplish and why. It also guides the activities of the plan, as everything in the plan should support the guiding principles of the charter. The charter should contain four key components: problem or risk statement, goals and benefits, project scope, and business impact. The problem or risk statement describes the challenge or risk the business is facing. The goals and benefits describe what you are hoping to achieve with the changes to be implemented. These goals should be specific and include targets that can be measured. The project scope describes what you will be planning to execute and deliver in order to reach the goals and benefits. The business impact describes what will be required in order to execute against the goal, and thus impacting cash, people, processes, technology and strategy. Creating the project charter helps ensure that proper thought has gone into what is to be accomplished and what it will take to get there.

High Level Roadmap: The high level roadmap should provide a simple picture of the key activities of the project that will yield impact to the business, along with key milestones. The roadmap should allow you to quickly communicate what will be taking place over the next X months. One of the keys to any successful project is to ensure you have quick wins and that you demonstrate early success. This will help keep the team motivated and make it easier to gain continued support for the project. While early wins and milestones are important, it's ok to have milestones further out in the future. In fact, the project may be broken into phases with more details surrounding the initial phase, and the later phases described in a conceptual state. Having a long term vision on the roadmap shows that you've thought through where the business goes next, with an expectation that the further out the plan goes, the more likely the plan may change.

Detailed Activity Plan: The detailed activity plan describes the specific tasks that need to happen for each component of the project. This should at minimum include target start and completion dates, owner of the task, any dependencies from other tasks and any resources required to complete the task (cash, technical or people). How you decide to create your detailed activity plan is up to you. Some businesses can be successful using a simple spreadsheet to organize their plan, others may have the resources and skills to use advanced project management software. The element I want to stress here is that you take the time to think through the steps required to execute the plan.

While there are endless ways to improve on your project plan, these are the three critical elements that I suggest you have in place to support success. Done right, these three elements give you what you will need to organize and execute. A final point worth mentioning is that before you execute your plan, you should share the charter and high level roadmap with your organization to gain their support and buy-in for the project. There will likely be some amount of change or impact to current business processes, and you want the entire organization open to change because they see the greater good and the long term benefit. This will drastically improve your success rate in executing. For example, if you are now asking customers to complete a survey after each transaction, some associates may find this task cumbersome, annoying and pointless since many customers will decline. However, if these associates understand why these surveys are important, then even if only a few customers actually complete them, associates will be more likely to execute as needed.

Tracking Against Your Plan

With a detailed plan now created and in execution mode, it will be important to track against the plan on a regular basis. You must set aside time to do this to ensure activities are progressing against the targets. Remember that each activity should have an owner, so there should be someone accountable to provide an update of progress. How often you need to review the plan will depend on how aggressive the plan is, but will likely be at least weekly. Depending on how complex the activities are and the competence of the activity owners, it may require a regular meeting amongst the entire team, or it could be as simple as email updates. While you'll need to determine the appropriate cadence based on your situation, I would not go more than 2 weeks without reviewing the project status. Anything beyond this and the project will have a high chance of getting lost or forgotten.

Measuring Your Results

As you progress through executing the project plan, there will be two important types of measurements to account for. The first is measurement against project milestones. This is relatively straight forward as when activities complete, they are marked on the detailed project plan. Communication of the milestones is just as important as measuring them. Be sure that those involved in achieving the milestones are recognized for their contributions. Not all milestones need to be on the project plan either when it comes to recognition. For example, let's suppose you're going to implement a new customer satisfaction survey to help improve attrition. The first milestone might be to setup a survey system that is ready to be presented to customers; certainly a milestone on the project plan and worth communicating. However, maybe you decide to announce when you've gotten your 100th customer survey submission. While not on the project plan, it helps the team and organization feel good that the efforts are paying off. Then, after your first analysis based on customer data you may decide to make a change to the product offering as a result of the survey. Again this should be communicated as another key result of everyone's participation.

This brings us to the second type of measurement, which is measurement of the health impact as a result of the project. Remember that the project goal should include measurable targets, and therefore, every activity that is desired to improve the health of the business should have a clear definition up front of how it will be measured to understand the health impact. Going back to the above example, when the product offering change produces positive impact to the business (for example, maybe total customer spend is now higher), communicate that victory and reinforce how the survey was a big part of that. This will build more confidence and continued support for the current and future business health projects.

Reassessment

The good news is that if you've followed the steps in this book, you'll soon be executing against a plan to improve the health of your business. It will be based on a solid understanding of your business, and you will have likely selected to focus on the areas that will have the biggest impact first. The bad news, however, is that your plan may not remain stable. Your business will find fluctuations that may cause you to need to shift gears. It's important to continually assess where your business is at based on the health rating. With that said, if a component of a project is near completion, finish it. Get the milestone victory and recognize that the work done will likely still yield positive health gains even if it's no longer the most critical concern. In fact, you may choose to complete every project activity in flight and merely alter or expedite future activities based on the latest health rating trends.

Continual reassessment is important so that you have a picture of where your risks are at all times. Contrary to what I said above, if a risk is substantially detrimental to your business, then there's nothing wrong with pausing everything in flight, if needed, to keep the business alive. However, try to avoid such drastic maneuvers if you can. Continue to focus on business health improvement and keep your plans, charters and roadmaps updated accordingly. As long as you are tracking and measuring your achievements, they are still worth celebrating; even the small victories.

RESEARCH RESULTS

In support of this book, I conducted a survey of 31 small business owners and leaders, ranging across various industries, sizes, revenue and time in business, to assess how well they understand the health of their business. My purpose for writing this book created the hypothesis that I was out to test, that most businesses are not properly measuring the health of their business. This section provides a closer look into the research collected.

The key take away from the research is that most businesses, as suspected, are not measuring the health of their business, at least in the way I suggest is required to achieve sustainable success throughout this book. In fact, the majority of businesses do not even collect the required metrics to not only measure business health, but to even just understand their customers. Per the responding businesses, less than 13% collect and measure the key customer metrics to support the health rating formula discussed within. These metrics include: number of new customers acquired, customer acquisition cost, long term customer value, average revenue per customer, and customer attrition. Of the few businesses that are collecting the right metrics, only half believe they have a significant understanding of the health of their business; meaning that just having the metrics is not necessarily enough, you must know how to apply the metrics to maximize their value. Even without the health monitoring process, these metrics provide key insights to understanding customers.

Despite the low percentage of businesses actually attaining the proper metrics, more than 56% of the businesses felt they had at least a sufficient understanding of the health of their business, if not a significant understanding. I believe this is one of the major disconnects that stifles business success. Businesses believe they understand their health, but they are not collecting the right information to possibly really understand it. Whether this results in business failure or limits growth will vary by company; but in either case it represents a clear opportunity for businesses to refocus their attention.

Respondents were also asked to quantify how many members of their company are dedicated to generating and analyzing customer analytics. The results for the most part are not that surprising. Companies with larger revenue and more employees were more likely to have at least one person focused on analytics. To that point, less than 40% of smaller companies (less than 50 employees or less than $10 million in revenue) have a dedicated focus on customer analytics. Interestingly, none of the companies in business less than 3 years had any focus on analytics. Maybe it takes a few years for a business to realize that analytics are needed to reach the next level or to stay in business. Could it be that many businesses realize this too late, after their business has closed or has no chance for survival? Or, maybe this is known by many businesses, but it's not until the business becomes more mature that the business can figure out how to actively focus on analytics.

While every business is unique, I believe there's a common theme in the need for more focus on customer analytics. With business failure rates so high, one must believe there's more to success than just luck. There is a way to better understand the direction your business is going, and as a result, get ahead of potential disaster.

While this study was not designed to prove that analytics has been the key factor in success for those businesses that are still surviving, it is extremely interesting that businesses that pass the 3 year mark are more likely to have focus on analytics than those starting off. I know I am not alone in my belief that analytics are a key ingredient to business success, as there are hundreds of books and articles that support this belief. The ultimate question is whether small businesses will come to believe in the value of analytics and take action to make analytics part of their everyday business practice...before it's too late.

What is clear, however, is that many businesses operate today admitting that they minimally understand the health of their business. At the same time, most businesses fail to collect the metrics and generate the analytics that fuel the formulaic approach to forecasting business health presented here. Based on the study results, I stand by my belief that an opportunity exists to improve business success rates, and the concepts of this book provide a valid approach to make that happen.

Made in the USA
Middletown, DE
25 July 2015